DIVINE ENCOUNTER

Divine Encounter

Copyright © 2019 Brian Guerin

ISBN: 9781093274608

All rights reserved. No part of this book may be used or reproduced by any means, graphic, electronic, mechanical, including photocopying, recording, taping, or by any information storage retrieval system without the written permission of the author except in the case of brief quotations embodied in critical articles and reviews.

The Holy Bible, English Standard Version® (ESV®) Copyright © 2001 by Crossway, a publishing ministry of Good News Publishers. All rights reserved.

*Cover design, typeset, development by PTP publishing co.

|| Printed in the United States of America

DIVINE ENCOUNTER

BRIAN GUERIN

CONTENTS

Introduction	vii
1. Definitions and Divinity	1
2. Apologetics and Answers	11
3. Plans and Purposes	21
4. Initiations and Installments	35
5. Commissionings and Callings	49
6. Surprises and Suddenlies	61
7. Covenant and Contingencies	67
8. Contention and Conflict	75
9. Methods and Models	87
10. Revealings and Relocations	93
11. Empowerment and Expansion	105
12. Encounters and Experiences	117
Prayer for Encounters	141
About the Author	143

INTRODUCTION

My expectation with this book is that both while reading and after reading, you'll have run-ins with God you've never had before that will shift *everything*. My whole life up to this point has gone through this window—this vein of divine encounter, if you will. It's what we really long for and hunger for: to intimately *know Him* and *encounter Him*. Yet the encounter itself isn't the sole focus of our pursuit; what the encounter *produces* most importantly, is what we're going after—not just the *wow* of it all. What divine encounters produce is more important than the encounter itself.

Throughout this work, we'll be covering what many of these encounters are intended for, where they come from, and the various facets of their existence in our lives. I'm going to be dropping plenty of Scripture for a theological foundation, but I can tell you ahead of time, we'll also share plenty of stories, not just from the Scriptures, but from my personal life as we go.

Our aim is for this realm to break open into our world. That's how heaven works: the more you mull over, mediate, and turn your attention to certain aspects of the Kingdom, the more it opens up to touch us and flip our world upside down.

May the reality of an experiential God be yours as you work your way through these pages. Let the truths, principles, and stories within motivate and propel you into a place of consistent encounter that leaves you changed in an irreversible way.

1

DEFINITIONS AND DIVINITY

ENCOUNTERS IN SIMPLE TERMS

divine *(adjective)*: *of* or *from* God
encounter *(verb)*: to *come upon* or *meet with*, especially *unexpectedly*

The definition above spells out clearly how many encounters with God happen: *unexpectedly*. While you can seek after and fight diligently for these encounters and run-ins with Him, when He comes, typically, you can never figure it out when and how it will take place.

In Acts 2, it says they knew Jesus told the disciples to wait until they were endued with power from on high. So the 120 went into the upper room and were consistently locked up in prayer together. *Expectation* was there and they knew what they were going after. They didn't quite know *what* they were getting into with the encounter or *when* it was coming. Encounters with God are like that; they come unexpectedly, and I personally love that. But the 120 obeyed the voice of God and pursued it diligently, and their hunger and pressing in triggered an encounter. You don't always have to know when or how... but we must know the *what* we are going after.

The Scripture says they were all continually in prayer in the upper room, and then suddenly the sound of the mighty rushing wind came, snuck up on them, overturned their world, and everything was flipped upside down from one encounter. At Pentecost, the Holy Spirit first being poured out flipped the world upside down and trickled down into what you and I walk in *even* today.

This is a true definition and example of *divine* and *encounter* coming together. My definition is a *supernatural experience*. Everything in the Kingdom manifests itself through faith, belief, hunger, and expectancy. Let's start off with laying the groundwork and build a faith and expectancy while also crushing the religious spirit that tries to hinder what we're going for.

What is a divine encounter experience? I would define it as such: *a supernatural experience that invades your natural world for God's ultimate purposes and plan; a divine run-in with God that literally alters your entire destiny and life call.* This definition is intentionally broad because God is so broad and multifaceted in His approach to mankind. His approach to move to, in, and through mankind is broad.

That's why the word divine is "of" or "from" God. It doesn't always have to be *God Himself*. It starts getting complex from the other side, but it's basically a supernatural *break-in* into the natural that has so many different reasons for God's purposes. It's all throughout Scripture from the Old Testament to the New. All over the earth you can see the hunger that we're having in this day and hour —we've got to walk in experience with God like never before.

I'm grateful for all we've tapped into and all we are walking up to this day, but there's much more to be experienced. I'd encourage you to always be in that same stance and posture, a standpoint of gratefulness. The Bible talks of entering into His courts with thanksgiving and praise, and always contending, because there is a fullness out there that we're ever chasing.

This stirs me up. I am constantly contending for a fresh, new run-in with God like never before. I don't care where you're at in life. I don't care if you just got born again yesterday or you've been in this thing for ten years, or you're in the marketplace ministry, it's all a level playing field. We've all got to experience Him for greater endowment, commissioning, revelation, and transition. These encounters have so much impacted, that once they hit you, everything changes.

THE VALUE OF ENCOUNTERS

Why are divine encounters so important? Simply put: it's the way God set this whole thing up; He is an experience-able God. You've got to catch this: God is a God of relationship, He's a God of encounter, and He's a God of *experience*. If it's not about relationship, encounter, and experience—it isn't the God of the Bible.

You see, religion typically will tell you otherwise. I had this fed to me as well, and I still hear it to this day. Many leaders and pastors have bashed us. We still love them and bless them. We have these schools for the Bride where those who are so hungry come from all over the nations.

We hear everywhere we go; that people can sense and feel that there is more than Sunday morning church services. There's nothing wrong with church gatherings; I'm in them all the time preaching. However, there is more! There's a deep hunger raising up in the heavens right now. That's what we really want to go for in the land and help us all to rise up in this hour like never before.

So, to get back to the question, why is divine encounter so important? Because beginning in the book of Genesis all the way through Revelation, we can see this is literally the way God has structured His connection to humanity; through experience, encounter, and relationship. It's His nature.

Another reason why we must live in and out of *divine encounter* is because you can only impart what has been personally imparted to you. This is big; knowledge and second-hand preaching of sermons and things we've heard can only get us so far. But divine encounter actually imparts and empowers a substance in which you can then release to others. This is very, very paramount. I actually learned this by accident.

I got born again at the age of twenty (I'm thirty-nine at

the time of writing this). I was really zealous for the Lord and fasting/praying on this journey. I knew very little but I knew I had met Jesus and I was in love with Him. Very soon after that I went off to Bible college. I experienced profound power, not so much prophetic—a little bit of that—but this was the Brownsville Revival, a true outpouring of the Holy Spirit. Wonders and signs everywhere. It was crazy. I spent two years raised up in this. But again, I don't care who you're under, who you run with, or who you know. If you personally don't have a run-in with God, it's okay. You're born again, destiny can still happen, but I'm just trying to stir hunger and encourage you to encounter God one-on-one. You don't have to be in the five-fold ministry or anything like that. But I saw some amazing things during this time of my life in Bible college. I saw the power of God as we'd pray for people and they'd get healed. We saw fruit.

But I graduated Bible school and there was that stirring that I'm feeling again even now as I write this book, that *there's more*. I'm just hungry. I don't know if I know what it is, but I'm hungry in a very good way. But at that time in my life, I felt this hunger come on me and it just would not get off me. I would wake up in the morning and go to bed at night and just knew I *needed* Jesus. So I started searching through Scripture, and thank God for some men of God I was learning from, but these things just started being highlighted to me in God's Word, things I'll touch on later in this book.

I began to see this common thread through Scripture of these men and women who would encounter God and everything would change. Moses was shepherding his father-in-law's sheep, which was pretty mundane, and then *boom*, he ran into a burning bush, then delivered all of Israel. Joshua was under Moses for some time, and knew the presence of God, then they crossed over the Jordan River and the angel of the Lord of hosts took out Jericho. Then there's Gideon, a coward (see Judges 6), and an angel comes to him and makes him a mighty man of God and a hero to Israel.

I saw this common thread with these run-ins and many other run-ins, these divine encounters men and women had that changed everything. When I saw this, I thought, *Oh, that's it!* because up until this point, I had experienced enough of God and was madly in love with Him. I began to see this common thread in all these encounters, and I couldn't help but realize it's how God set it up.

This isn't to make you feel condemned if you haven't had an encounter with God, but to make you hunger for one. Even before regularly encountering God, I would watch this common thread I saw in the Scriptures and see how destiny and life would shift all around these encounters.

So I began to cry out to God because I knew I had to encounter Him. I saw it was the biblical pattern to have a hunger for a one-on-one run-in with God, I don't care who you are, who you've trailed, who you've been an assistant to, none of that matters. It's a divine run-in with God. What do you do when you've had an encounter with God? Have another one. It's just an opening up of His nature and His Kingdom more and more that empowers you, gives you greater authority, and allows you to transform more into His likeness and start soaring through life. I began to see that He's a very experiential God, and it set me off on a journey where I locked a hold of the horns of the altar and I wasn't coming off of it, period. When I found out that "*this is that,*" this was not optional for me.

Let me encourage you, God's very sovereign and very loving, but He also rewards diligence. Hebrews says He's a rewarder of those who diligently seek Him, and His eyes run to and fro the earth looking for hearts that are fully after Him (see Hebrews 11:6). Hunger is one thing that God cannot overlook, I can tell you. Faith, expectancy, and hunger catch the attention of God. The Bible really says that if you ask in faith, you can just about have anything you ask. Of course, the request has to be in line with the Word of God. But God can't pass up hunger.

To reinforce how you can only impart what has been imparted to you, let me share this. I once had an experience, and personally, I didn't know what I was getting into, but it left a substance on me in this particular encounter. Before I knew it, everybody I'd get around started having dreams and visions. I'd go into meetings and talk about whatever, and all of a sudden I'd pray, and the common theme was these people were having dreams and visions.

That which you tap into in *secret*, will manifest in *public*. Anything you personally contend for and break open in the secret place in intimacy will by default start overlapping in public. You can't work this up, and don't have to even if you could. You'll see the difference in people that haven't experienced a whole lot in the secret place, and that's okay too.

We're all at different places, but I'm simply trying to stir up a hunger in you if that applies to you. Often those encounters will be very uniquely designed for your calling, which is beautiful of God. You can't pick what kind of encounter you want—it's got to be handpicked and carved out for your call and destiny.

At this time early on, I started noticing things. The stuff that I would run into by encounter would come upon and had been imparted to me. Then, whenever I was around other people it was just effortlessly imparted to them, no matter what their call was. It's really incredible.

A great example is the difference you'll see with ministers. Often you'll see some who may teach on the same topic, but one of them is teaching from experience and encounter versus another who's teaching from principles. Both are needed, but you start to see the difference is usually between ministers that minister out of encounter and experience, and that there's a substance there and an impartation that can be released from that substance. Whereas teaching from a sheer theological or intellectual standpoint when you've not had a run-in encounter, unless it's a sovereign move of God, you typically won't see an impartation of the very thing being taught on. That's the major difference. The net result of personal encounter is a manifestation of public encounter.

Say for example you hear different ministers that teach on angels and the angelic realm who've had encounters, experiences, manifestations, and the angelic involvement will start breaking out and increasing in other people's lives through their ministry. Whereas others may be just teaching from a scriptural standpoint but without much experience on it. I'm not trying to say anybody's right or wrong here, but experience is very important to encounter an impartation. That's why you see Elisha wouldn't allow Elijah out of his sight till he passed the mantle. It came straight from him. Of course, Elisha shadowed him during his entire apprenticeship, but even up until the end, he wanted Elijah's mantle. There are certain things you carry and can impart in the same way that they were *imparted* to you.

KNOWLEDGE WITHOUT EXPERIENCE

Knowledge *sans* experience is often much less fruitful than knowledge *with* experience. This is why I encourage you to encounter the Word of God; when stuff in the Scriptures stirs you up, camp out on it and ask God for it. Tell Him, *I want that for me in this area*, or *Make it real to me, Lord*. Whether it be by revelatory encounter, divine run-in with God, ask Him to make it real in an experiential way.

First Corinthians 8:1 says, "Knowledge puffs up but love builds up." I know the Bible also says, "Study to show thyself approved" (see 2 Tim 2:15), but it also says in 2 Cor 3:6, "The letter alone kills, but the Spirit brings life." We see knowledge of the letter versus the Spirit, which is the experience side of the letter. So knowledge alone kills. We need the letter plus the Spirit (experience). *That* is what brings life. It's the difference from the orthodox Jews—they have the same Old Testament we do, but it's complete death since they don't have Christ or the Holy Spirit living in them. It's the letter alone, and it kills. There's no experience there.

We don't minimize knowledge; we have to have it as well. The Bible says study to show ourselves approved, but the experiential aspect of it is all that I'm getting at. Knowledge puffs up, but love builds up. What is love? It's experiential. We need the knowledge, but accompanied with the experience of love in order to really be fruitful. Our pursuit of knowledge has to be accompanied by a pursuit of experience, otherwise—we are missing the points of knowledge and revelation to begin with.

2

APOLOGETICS AND ANSWERS

ANSWERING RELIGIOUS OBJECTIONS

We've laid out a Word foundation in the previous chapter about divine encounters. Whether it's the upper room in Acts 2 or the impartation of grace with Elijah and Elisha, you can't escape encounters when reading the Scriptures. Yet despite these things, you may hear the religious counter it. You personally may be far past this, but others reading this may not be, as we're all in different places. As a result, I think it's important to stop for a moment to annihilate this so you can encounter the *fullness of what God wants* in the following pages.

If you think you're going to know God personally on a deep level and portray Him in the earth in His full glory without experience, I'm sorry, but that's just unbiblical. It's not in the book I read. But religion has this masterful way of putting these lenses over people's eyes that read the same book you and I do, but they walk out this life that's void of these encounters. Again, I'm not trying to be disrespectful. I hope you can read my heart in this. I bless them and I'll meet with anyone on whatever level they'll let me get to, so it's not that I think anybody is greater than anybody else. It's just that we want the fullness of God and what He's really mapped out for us. I'm just trying to call *everybody* higher.

One of the main objections you'll hear from a religious spirit is, "We don't go by feelings and experiences; we just go by the Word of God, brother. We walk by faith, not by sight." Or, "We don't need experiences; that's why He left us the written Word."

I've heard this said many times; you might have as well. The problem with it, is that the written Word of God is full of experience and true faith. They say they're not walking by sight but walking by faith, but true biblical-originated faith *always* leads to experience, encounter, and relationship. It sounds like a nice spiritual-sounding cliché, packaged with quoted verses, but it's actually not biblical at all.

Let's start at the very beginning of the book with the very first encounter, and all the way to the end, and look at some passages in between. The very first encounter of God to man is when He created man, of course, but then God breathed His breath into him. The *ruach* Spirit of God into man's nostrils created life from well-shaped dirt. The very first account God ever had with man was a full-out encounter, supernatural and divine. Then fast-forward a little bit, and God's walking in the cool of the day with Adam. God's very experiential; He loves to manifest Himself and loves to encounter His people. Religion hates that and wants Him out of it. Religion typically has a profound *anointing*, for lack of a better term, for using the *book* to *oust* the very Author of it.

I've seen this happen time and again, and a lot of it is rooted in fear of being deceived. It's based on people who have gone off into a ditch spiritually. Perhaps people have truly gotten off, but that doesn't mean the solution is to then put up such a religious barrier that you don't experience the fullness God intended for us. But the objectors will literally use the Word of God to block out the experience of God Himself, the very Author of it! You've got to be careful not to do that. That which you fear, you automatically become subject to, so anything you fear, you wind up giving dominance over your life to. So if you fear deception, you become deceived. Even though it may be a religious spirit, you still become deceived and limited from the fullness that God intends through experience and encounter, relationship and intimacy.

We need to always fear and revere God alone, trusting in Him and the Holy Spirit to guide us in His full ways, then you stay in the fullness. But the religious spirit just says, "We walk by faith, not by sight," and offers no true encounter.

So the encounter blueprints start with Adam being breathed to life, and ends in the book of Revelation, which was written *from* an encounter. You crack open the Bible, and God's first interaction with man is a full-out encounter experience. You close out the book with Revelation, and that whole book is written based on a divine encounter where John ascends up to heaven, and Jesus is writing letters for

John to give to angels of the churches. This is a full-out revelation by *experience*! Not to mention all of the encounters and happenings that are sandwiched between Genesis and Revelation.

TRUE FAITH LEADS TO *AUTHENTIC* EXPERIENCE

I've heard it said, "You don't need experience; be careful brother, even the elect can be deceived; you don't need an encounter, that's why God left us the written Bible." But see, God left us a written Word to allow us to see what all these biblical figures tapped into. The Word is an invitation! It's not merely a record, but happenings that can be duplicated.

Oh my goodness, a burning bush! Are you kidding me? Paul seeing a blinding light. Jesus seeing open heavens! The cloud of witnesses are all on the other side, looking at us—that's why it's in there in the written Bible: to urge you that God is no respecter of persons. He wants to encounter you like the saints of old, yet in a unique way.

There was only one burning bush, so that's another problem with the religious. When they hear you talk of an encounter, they might ask you, "Where is that in the Bible?" Well, where was the precedent for the burning bush when Moses encountered it? It had never happened before, nor since. What about Paul's blinding light? God is so creative and vast, when He encounters mankind, He can almost not even repeat the same encounter. He's too creative, full, and vast. He is full of variety and mystery. So when He encounters mankind in almost every single one of the Scriptures, the only time you see similarities is with predecessors.

With Moses and the burning bush, he was told to take off his shoes. The Lord of Hosts appeared to Joshua, and the same thing was said, "Take off your shoes." Both Moses and Joshua split bodies of water. With Moses it was the Red Sea, and Joshua the Jordan River. Elisha split the water with the mantle just like his mentor Elijah did. You'll see predecessors have similar encounters, but other than that, not many encounters are repeated the same way throughout Scripture.

That's why I want to encourage you when you hear a religious person tell you, "Watch out, don't get deceived!" we've got to realize who we're dealing with here; the God of all the universe who's so vast and who created all the galaxies that we still haven't even figured out. Not to mention the depths of the sea and creatures in it we still haven't discovered and maybe never will ... and we think we can confine Him to, "Where's that in the Bible?"

The end of the gospel of John says that if all the things Jesus did during His earthly ministry were recorded, there wouldn't be enough books in the world to contain it all. He was just one Man ministering and having encounters/experiences for 3.5 years. Imagine what encounters are available to us!

Stir yourself up for experience and encounter. Don't let religion talk loudly and say, "Well, that's just for the super saints." No, it's not at all. It's for everybody, all mankind, and it's meant to be *common*.

Real biblical faith always leads to experience and

encounter. It's the substance of things hoped for and not seen (see Hebrews 11:1). Yet it also taps into that which is seen, otherwise it's not even real faith. Abraham is dubbed the father of our faith. If anybody knows it better than everybody else, it would be him. You can check out Hebrews 11, the Hall of Faith, which details all the heavyweights of faith. All of them had authentic faith that produces literal encounters and manifestations. They were not confined by religion or a fear of becoming imbalanced.

THE FACE OR THE HAND?

God is not uncomfortable with you pressing in for Him to encounter you. That's how He set this up. One of the main lies you'll hear when you encounter religion, when you're talking about encounter and experience is, "Seek God's face and not His hand." But in reality, we're supposed to seek *everything* of God. Jesus told us to seek the Kingdom, for example. Was He wrong because He didn't say seek His face? See, it all points back to Him anyway. He's not nervous about any of this. That inherent hunger you feel, well, He created it in you to want to experience Him. That's why mankind is so hungry for the supernatural—they want to have an experience with God and want to walk with Him in the cool of the day.

Abraham brought Isaac up on the mountain by faith. What did his faith do? Caused experience. They encountered a ram with its horns caught in the thicket. A full-blown supernatural encounter. Then of course, an angelic encounter followed. That's where faith led Abraham; to experience. Faith always leads to experience, so people who say, "Well, we don't need to encounter or experience anything. It's not about what we feel. It's about faith."

About six or seven years ago, I was waiting upon the Lord. I still remember the exact chair I was sitting in, and I slipped into a vision where I saw Abraham's hand in the air about to make a sacrifice. I saw that Abraham's hand was shaking, and this really caught me by surprise, as I was just spending time with the Lord and He wanted to highlight and show me some things. Faith is not always attached to emotions. Faith is a decision to obey God, and what the voice of God told you. A lot of times we think faith needs to be attached to the right emotion, but I'm seeing Abraham shaking his hand nervously, and he's probably having doubts. Faith also doesn't mean there's no doubt there, either. It's not the full absence of doubt; it's just submission to faith over doubt by obedience.

Nevertheless, Abraham was willing to go through with it. In Hebrews 11, it says he was already trusting that God would raise Isaac from the dead, who the very promise he received was supposed to come through. But there's a ram caught in a thicket instead. He experienced a full-out provisional encounter by faith, as Hebrews states.

Sarah herself received power to conceive, even when she was past her age (Hebrews 11:11). By faith Enoch walked with God and was taken (Hebrews 11:5). Are you reading this? Experience after experience after experience! Attached to what? Faith.

So for all these religious folks who say, "Well, we just walk by faith and don't need to experience God," that's funny, because 100 percent of the time, biblical faith leads to *experience*. Abraham, by faith: ram in the thicket. Sarah, by faith: pregnant at ninety-nine years old. Enoch by faith: taken by God for crying out loud! By faith, the Red Sea split and the Israelites walked out in freedom on dry land. By faith the walls of Jericho fell once encircled seven times. On and on and on, experiences are caused by faith, not a substitute for faith, as the religious might say. They often use the Bible to set up a religious parameter that's not really biblical and ostracizes God and the movement of the Holy Spirit, which is pretty dangerous.

Imagine Israel walking around five, six, seven days around Jericho. It's still by faith. Imagine the objections: *Yeah right! These big old walls as thick as they are high are going to come tumbling down? Not a chance!* And sure enough, on the seventh day they did because they obeyed. They probably didn't feel it, because to reiterate, faith usually doesn't have emotions at all. Usually doubt seems like it's bigger, but if you're obeying faith, faith's bigger. That which you *obey* becomes *bigger* in your life.

So you have God speaking to you on the one hand, but fear is talking to you on the other, and it feels like fear is louder. In that case, always submit and obey the voice of the Lord, and you'll be okay—even though the other voice seems louder. Doubt can put on a big front by often playing on your mind, your will, and emotions, but as long as your steps are following His voice, it's accredited as righteousness by faith in God and you'll see promises come to fruition.

I felt it necessary in these early chapters to get religion out of the way because the slightest kink in this thing can really hinder experiencing God. You'll be limited if that small, antagonizing voice is still there saying, *Well, this may be for these people, but not me;* or, *I'm just gonna walk by faith 'cause I don't need experience, bless God!*

So I agree, let's walk by faith, but also walk in the encounter that stems from faith. Faith leads to encounter, experience, and transition. It has *substance*. No amount of religion that you can possibly pile on has the ability to put down a person who's full of faith and set on experiencing the living God Himself.

3

PLANS AND PURPOSES

THE WHY BEHIND THE TOUCH

We're going to go into more detail and camp out on a few of these encounters later in the book, but I wanted to share a brief list of biblical encounters that we all might be familiar with. Reason being, if these saints, and even Jesus Himself, had tangible encounters from heaven, don't you think we could use them as well?

- Moses and the burning bush.
- Joshua and the Angel of the Lord of hosts.
- Gideon and the commissioning by angelic encounter.
- Elijah called up in a whirlwind only to drop his mantle to Elisha.
- Isaiah, caught up in a vision, seeing the Lord and the train of His robe filling the temple.

- Ezekiel gets caught up between the heavens and the earth to see visions of God.
- Paul and the blinding light in Acts 9.
- Peter and the Mount of Transfiguration with Jesus.
- Peter has a trance and receives his call to the Jews in Acts 10:10.
- John gets caught up and writes the book of Revelation.
- Philip is supernaturally transported in the book of Acts.
- Jesus sees open heavens.

If anybody *didn't* need divine encounters, it would have been Jesus. I'm sorry, but Jesus' whole earthly life and ministry is full of encounters; walking on water, angels ministering to Him twice, a cloud of witnesses coming to Him on the Mount of Transfiguration (Moses and Elijah instructing Him). Continually in prayer He would see the Father and what He was doing first; prayed all night to pick the disciples. Even Jesus started His ministry with heavens opened up and the Holy Spirit descended upon Him like a dove, and commissioned Him off into the wilderness, which led to Him coming back in the power of the Spirit.

All of these are supernatural encounters, from commissionings to transitions, mantle passing, axe heads floating, Elisha and his assistant's eyes being fully opened, to angelic encounters—this was in a battle season, and they needed this so they had more angels on their side than the number of their enemies.

So for that reason I have a problem when people say, "Just stick to the Word of God," when the written Scriptures themselves are full of such encounters! Men and women that walked on this earth continually encountering God that helped guide and empower them for God's purposes. The book is full of encounter, all over the New Testament—with the exception of the epistles, you don't see a whole lot of that because they're letters to the churches; these are more instructional. But anywhere where you see minor and major prophets in the Old Testament, the book of Acts, Revelation, the Gospels—it's all experiential. I just want to encourage you to get a new outlook on Scripture, and see that God wants to jump out of this book and encounter us.

Some of you reading this have had encounters, while others haven't. Some, like myself, have had plenty in our lives but are longing for more. There's no end of God with experience and encounters. And the thing about it is the more you encounter God, the more you become like Him. You become more empowered to fulfill His purposes as a result of visitation. The resulting fruit from these encounters is never ending.

God is longing to encounter each and every one of us no matter what our ultimate destiny may be. You may be the housewife, the missionary, a businessman, full-time minister, school principal, teacher, or lawyer. God is no respecter of persons and longs to encounter all. The Bible says that He is the same yesterday, today, and forever (see Hebrews 13:8). If

He encountered the saints long ago throughout the Old Testament all the way throughout the New, He's longing to still encounter His people. And much more so this day, I feel, like the last part of the race while preparing the Bride for His Son.

This whole thing is for two purposes: first and foremost, to intimately know God and walk with Him; secondly, to be used by God to touch humanity so they can intimately walk with Him and know Him. It's reciprocal of His Kingdom in a multifaceted way through the five-fold ministry, and through the training of the saints for the work of the ministry. But first and foremost, this whole thing is about loving God intimately and becoming one with Him. Then, spreading His good news so others can do the same. This is even why Jesus is the Bridegroom and the Church is the Bride. The spiritual blueprint of it is in heaven of course, but we even see it in the natural with a husband and wife.

If you have a husband and wife who ride out their marriage covenant solely based on their marriage license/contract and not experience any relational run-ins and encounters, then you've got a serious problem. So if God set this whole thing up in His image, then let's look at it in reverse. Typically we go by heaven's blueprint, and then mimic it on earth in the natural. But for the sake of ease, let's flip that around and look at the earth.

He created man in His image, and you see man and woman become one and the relationship is based upon, of course, some of the letter, the license (contract), and the sheer ethics, legitimacy, and other fundamentals of the relationship. But also one huge facet that you can't do away with: experience of love, encounter, and empowerment one to the other, just like Jesus does to the church.

Imagine seeing a husband and wife who communicate like the religious crowd today. "Hey babe, meet you at the courthouse! Let's ink it up today and sign the marriage license. That way we can make this thing official!" Then they sign the license, and just get in both their cars and go their separate ways. Before departing one says to the other, "Make sure you get your copy because we don't live by experience, we've got the written contract!" We'd think that's ridiculous, because *it would be*.

I get it, we're saved through grace by faith, and that's a strong aspect of this. But again, if you just solely rely on your walk and relationship upon a contract alone, fold it up and throw it in your glove box, how well will you know that person and their heart? Will you become one with them and know them personally, and also produce fruit that's going to change others? It's just how God set this whole thing up. He's very experiential. We don't limit our experience in other earthly contracts. So why do we do so with a heavenly covenant?

Not experiencing Him and trying to have a relationship with Him is like ordering food but not eating it. If you think about everything we do in life—the smells, sounds, the animals, the trees, the wind, the weather pattern—everything God set up (even drinking coffee!) is experiential. So if we take it back to the origin, God's very into experiencing you and encountering you. No matter where you're at in life, no matter how many mistakes you've made in the past, God is very loving and He longs to encounter you.

When Adam fell, God was the first one there with, "Adam, where are you?" He loved to walk in the cool of the day with Adam. God loves to woo His people by experience. He's the God who manifested His glory in the temple so thick, the priest couldn't stand to minister as there was way too weighty of a shekinah glory in the air. He was a pillar of cloud by day and a fire by night. He loves to manifest His glory and presence. Encounters that happen are revelatory, experiential, and/or angelic.

There are a number of avenues by which encounters take place:

- The Father
- The Son
- The Holy Spirit

The Trinity first and foremost is the means by which we encounter Him. The Godhead can manifest for different reasons and purposes. You see the Father appearing to Christ (Matthew 3:17), Christ appearing to Paul (Acts 9), and the Holy Spirit appearing to the church (Acts 2). There are a handful of other encounters that we see in the Word which came by and through:

- Angelic beings
- The cloud of witnesses

PURPOSES

1) FRESH COMMISSIONING

The biblical way to commission people by God is through encounter. Does it always have to be that way? No, but it's extremely common. The Lord is famous for launching ministries, exploits, missions, trips, transitions, and journeys through encounter.

2) EMPOWERMENT

Without question, encountering God gives you the ability to do what you could not do before. We see this repeatedly throughout Scripture.

Look at Saul in 1 Samuel 10. Saul was just a regular guy until the prophet Samuel came and prophesied the word of the Lord over him and commissioned him as king over Israel. The text says, "He turned," and then the Spirit of God came upon Saul (see 1 Samuel 11:16). That's the divine encounter. The text says Saul became a new man (1 Samuel 10:6). The Scripture says that God gave him a brand-new heart and was totally transformed in an instant because he had a divine encounter where the Spirit of God came upon him. He reigned powerfully until he went off-track later.

It's worth noting again that divine encounters don't happen in the natural. Of course, you can have divine appointments set up by God, but we're not really talking about that. We are talking about divine encounters that step through from the other side into this one, and absolutely flipping your destiny upside down, with empowerment, commissioning, and complete upheaval *in a good way* for the purposes of God.

In the earth, there's plenty of divine setups and happenings, and I love those too. For example, someone walking up and handing you a check for the exact amount you needed to pay your light bill. But that's not what I'm referring to here. So again, a divine encounter is God stepping through that side into this one, bringing the supernatural into the natural and doing so in a way that only He can do in His ways. It's really a beautiful design because it makes us so dependent upon Him. We can't do anything without the Holy Spirit, just like how Jesus told His disciples not to leave Jerusalem until they were endued with power from on high (Luke 24:49). We can't do anything without God. Encounters breed empowerment.

The power to walk out the call comes in the encounter. That's another thing, too, that I love about experiencing God; you can't walk in a certain authority of a calling if you aren't ordained by the Lord, and sent by Him. Good luck fulfilling a divine commission without divine help. It's going to be forced, and it's not going to have authority on it. You may object to my saying that by thinking of the Scripture that says we're to go out into all the world, and we can. But also, Paul, in Acts 16 was wanting to go into certain regions with the Gospel. If we read closely, we see it says the Spirit of Jesus resisted them from going into Phrygia. This is also how keen they knew the voice of God in the triune Godhead, which to me is incredible. They understood that certain regions required a certain grace to labor in.

If you go in what you're not commissioned to and try to operate in something that's not your call, God is gracious and merciful, but you can tell there's just not an ease on it, there's not an authority; it's forced. There's just real biblical precedent for being commissioned in Acts 16. Then Paul has the dream of the Macedonian and they go to Macedonia in authority, fruit, and power.

3) REVELATION

Simply put, revelation gives the understanding we need. It provides the know-how. This is the wisdom to govern the various facets of life that God would have us influence.

4) TRANSITION (REPOSITIONING)

Divine encounters come when you've been going in one direction by God's calling, but then it's time to shift position and transition for a new purpose He has for you. In this case, He'll hit you with another encounter and it will shift everything with a new authority, vision, and focus.

One of the main things I want to point out with experiences with God is there's typically never one final encounter that sums up your whole call. I love this about God; He's so vast and full. There are actually *installments*, and that's why we will have *transitioning* or *repositioning* encounters. I'm just being honest with you; a lot of times I've had this mindset that once your set call is say a certain thing, even in the five-fold ministry, which it doesn't even have to be in, then that's what you are *for life*. That's not really biblical. I'm sure you'll carry that aspect and authority the rest of your life, but you can shift into other areas of ministry. Another thing I want to point out is when I talk about this we're definitely not talking about just the five-fold ministry. I've seen commissionings happen in the marketplace just like in the ministry place.

I remember even in Bible college what was before me all the time was one of the most world-renowned evangelists to date and so by default and by sheer nature, I wanted to be an evangelist. Lo and behold, heaven sideswiped me with this encounter years later that totally took me on another path. I still ended up in what we would call *ministry*, but really, ministry in its purest form is obeying Jesus. It's not somebody behind a pulpit with one of the five-fold titles.

Another thing that's been skewed in church, and I know the intentions behind why it's taught are well-meaning, but everybody says, "God first, family second, ministry third." I know what they mean, so please hear me out in this, but I've heard that for quite a number of years and it's not completely accurate. Again, not to get technical, and please don't go to your church and tell them how off this is. I'm not trying to be a spiritual police.

True ministry, if you want to call it that, in its purest form is the first two commandments; love God first and foremost, and love your neighbor as yourself. And Jesus taught that if you love Him, you'll obey Him. So you can't separate the two. You cannot practically say, *God first, family second, ministry third.* I know what the people who say this mean; they mean it as if ministry is a profession and don't put your family after it. *I get all that.* Jesus said even if you love your father or mother more than Him then you're not worthy of the Kingdom. It doesn't have to be this weird thing, because if you are in pure, true ministry of obeying God, and loving Him, by default you're going to love your family to the fullest and you're going to raise up in the fullness of all He is. So it's not about obeying this perfect systematic priority order. It's about obeying and loving God, and as a result, the rest will fall into place.

The last thing I want to see is for us as a people to box ourselves in with a calling or some arbitrary ministry list. I'm telling you, there are so many unique and ornate niches of the Kingdom God's trying to fill, and so many people are trying to be like Apostle Paul, when they may be a Timothy.

And what happens is we're called to be Timothy but we're trying to step into a Paul, and the authority and grace is not there. As a result we keep running up against walls, there's no favor, and doors get shut. Nobody is any greater than any other. We don't have to try to fit a calling that isn't ours. When it's the will of God for you, it's like a circle peg in a circle hole, it fits perfectly. You'll start to notice this on our calls and destiny that if you get outside of who you truly are as designed by God, you become a square peg in a circle hole that doesn't fit. Far too often I think it's because people are seeing certain cookie-cutter roles that may be more on the forefront before us, and we're trying to force these pegs into the wrong-shaped hole. Just because God encountered you once with a specific call doesn't mean that call can't shift and change. Be open to encountering new plans, graces, and anointings during the soon-coming encounters you'll have with God.

SO IN CLOSING THIS SECTION, I JUST WANT TO REITERATE THAT God wants to encounter us powerfully and frequently. He really does. Often if we will posture ourselves in such hunger and set ourselves apart in wanting to encounter Him, He'll move at a rate that you can't even keep up with. Typically, you'd be surprised at how fast God's willing to move if we're willing to yield and posture ourselves correctly.

The other day I was talking with some friends about how the children of Israel were intended to go into the Promised Land in eleven days. That's to say their journey was supposed to be just an eleven-day journey, but because of decisions and choices and not posturing themselves right, they circled mountains for forty years. God doesn't intend that for any of us, but my point is, I think we often have this mentality that God moves slow or something, but it's usually slowness on our end, not His. He's wanting to encounter us and move in such profound ways at a really rapid pace, no matter what your call is. I've travelled much and I've seen it, trust me. Some of the most profound people running with God and having experiences aren't even behind pulpits, so one can't say these blessed encounters are for the super saints or five-fold ministry preachers. That has nothing to do with it.

Really, when this whole thing is wrapped up, rewards and delegating value in heaven are going to come down to who intimately *became one* with Him and obeyed Him most accurately. That's what it's really going to come down to.

In later chapters we'll get into more personal encounters, and I'll tie them in to Scriptures, but this is the groundwork I felt like we needed to establish first. These biblical foundations of faith clear the path and often allow us to dive into the depths of God, deception-free.

4

INITIATIONS AND INSTALLMENTS
RECOGNIZING SEASONS AND SHIFTS

Certain divine encounters don't sum up who you are for all of destiny. There are installments in your Christian life. In the natural, if someone started renting a new apartment, when you help them move in, as exciting as it is, you wouldn't necessarily expect that they are going to stay in that same apartment for their lifetime. Seasons will shift and change. Likewise, in the spirit, an encounter today might *superimpose* an encounter from yesterday.

Many people don't realize that in Acts 9 Paul had his initial encounter, his divine experience; blinding light from heaven, and a voice. When we get to Acts 13, we see Paul and Barnabas are running together, but they're referred to as teachers and prophets. A lot of people think Paul became the apostle Paul the moment he was hit with the blinding light on the way to Damascus. But there was a fourteen-year span of training and hearing revelations. He says in his writing he didn't even get the Gospel from any man. This dude was locked up with heaven, getting caught up in the mysteries. He even said "my Gospel" when he penned it. I even heard a minister say that he had an experience where he went to heaven and he ran into Paul, and he still calls it "his Gospel." Paul asked him, "Are they enjoying *my Gospel*?" He was so possessive of the revelation, not in an arrogant way but in a humble-ownership sort of way. I hear from people all the time ask questions like, "Well, you're a maverick. Who are you submitting to?" to which I answer, "Who was Paul submitting to?" He penned two-thirds of the New Testament by divine revelation from heaven.

So in Acts 13, Barnabas and Paul are really under the title of teacher and prophet. When we hop to the next chapter and it says they fasted and prayed and laid hands on them, this is another encounter or *installment*. It's a divine encounter, when it comes from that other world. Whether there's an installment, empowerment, transition, revelation, or in this case, it was a *repositioning* for Paul and Barnabas. It describes that the Holy Spirit came and sent them. He plucked them both out, as a prophet and teacher at the time, but the Holy Spirit sent them in the true definition of an apostle, a *sent one*. It was after this that they were referred to as apostles. Prior to that, they were prophets and teachers. This was an installment in their lives. It was a watershed moment where destiny shifted. Paul didn't get hung up on the initial title of prophet and teacher. He was open to a shift in ministry season.

I point this out because sometimes you can see somebody in a pastoral role commissioned by God for many years and then see them shift into the apostolic. Some of us watching can think they've gotten off or they're missing it. Not necessarily. These shifts are biblical and can certainly be of the Lord.

There's a modern-day prophet you may have heard of named Neville Johnson. He was the pastor of a large church for many years and then all of the sudden the Lord called him out and told him to give it all up and lock away with Him for some time, and the Lord opened up his eyes for six months to both the spiritual and natural world. When the season ended, he came out in a prophet role, and to this day as of this writing he operates as a full-blown prophet. Kenneth Hagin Sr. was a hardcore prophet. You'd look at him in his function and see he was very pastoral, but he was a prophet in function as well.

All that being said, I love experiences when God commissions a calling, but I also realize that there are installments along the way. Things can shift and change. But I must also encourage you not to feel like you have to have some profound experience. Some of the most powerful people I know have very little experiences. So never go off of that; that's never the gauge point.

My friend Todd White would be the first one to tell you he doesn't have a whole lot of experiences. He has told me before he's not seen much in the angelic or had a lot of dreams and visions and things, which really, to be honest with you, that's not abnormal for the call of an evangelist. The prophet, a mouthpiece for the voice of God, typically has more of the angelic messengers and things surrounding them. Not exclusively, but often a prophet will see various messages from God in the spirit. It's their role. So throughout this teaching, don't feel as though you're missing it if experiences aren't as dramatic as others. Repositionings and installments may come by simple means or a small voice in your spirit. Don't snag yourself on the idea that it must be an explosive, spectacular meeting with God.

No matter where you fall in this thing, allow me to encourage you to just go for it. Believe the Word of God and step out. I've seen it go too far into the ditch on either side. I've seen where people take it too far and force "supernatural" visitations, and on the other side there's folks who say we don't need angels or angelic encounter because we've got the Holy Ghost. Well, Jesus did, as did Peter and Paul. Peter got the Holy Ghost in Acts 2, but what about when he was locked up in Acts 12 and he needed an angel to free him? Or Paul at the end of the book of Acts? I've seen it go too far, and I don't want any readers of this book to do that. We want to remain childlike hungry and press in for the fullness of all these things.

I've seen the mentality where people think they're saved and have the Holy Spirit and don't need anything else as a result. On the surface, this is true. But again, if you look at true biblical examples—installments come repeatedly through the course of a *yielded* believer's life.

COMMISSION BY DEFINITION IS SIMPLY AN INSTRUCTION, command, or duty given to a person. So basically, it speaks of your assignment in life, but it doesn't mean that it's now exclusively your fixed call for life.

I would encourage you, ask Him, "What is my specific call? What I am here for?" And don't worry about what He's going to answer, because that doesn't always mean forever permanently fixed. There's shifts and seasons, and like I've been saying, there's installments, but a couple questions I would ask are, "What is my calling specifically?" "Who am I called to?" This is a big one. The Word says, "Ask of me and I will give you the nations as your inheritance" (Psalm 2:8).

So not only ask for a people or a nation but a city or neighborhood. Ask for your workplace. Ask for your street corner. As we discover these intricate callings, we'll walk in a more accurate level of obedience, but also with ease and authority. We need the Body of Christ all functioning in the fulness of what they're called for. We don't need a bunch of hands. We don't need a bunch of feet all hopping around. We need the fullness of the body.

So be open to whatever it may be for you. It may not be pulpit ministry. It might not be platform ministry. It may be the marketplace and not in front of lights or cameras. What's funny is if you thought you were supposed to be in a certain platform ministry and you're not, and you somehow get there anyway, you'll learn real quick what you really wanted —it will be hard, there'll be no grace on it, you'll be stressed out, you'll break under the pressure of the stress of certain things you thought you could handle. Trust me, you only want to be where God has you, and not only that, but that's where you're going to be the happiest, and you just don't care whatever it looks like. You just want to be wherever Jesus has you.

Again, I'd encourage you to openheartedly ask God what your specific DNA is in the Kingdom for that season and the years to come. What's that thumbprint He's branded you with for His purposes? And is there even a people group or a region maybe? Be open and press into this. You can't pick what your calling is. It was already set up and preordained, so you just need to find out what it is, seek God, and align with Him.

It's kind of like if we liken the Body of Christ to a baseball team. If you're a pitcher, and that's your call and gifting, then we don't need you in the outfield. You've got a strong arm, so please stand on the mound and pitch for the team. If you're an outfielder, we don't need you on the pitcher's mound. Traveling in ministry, I've seen where the pitcher might be the one seen most often, and a lot of people think they have to pitch, then. You may not realize your ornate call is to be in the outfield because you are way better than anybody else at that and that is what's going to make the *team* better. If that's the case, you're going to be a lot happier out there anyway because there's going to be a lot more ease and grace on it.

These divine encounters help reflect that and they speak to us about a course of action which enables us to hone in our specific callings, both seasonal, and lifetime. We don't need anybody in the Body getting out of their lane, so to speak, but we need for everybody to play their part. It's really key that we align ourselves in our true destiny and realize what we were born for. This will able us to cut the fat off of many areas of our lives. Far too often people are spread thin doing so many things that are Kingdom tasks, but God never told them to do two-thirds of it. Get rid of those two-thirds and focus on the one-third, and do it really well, and you'll start to see the favor and authority. You want to be where God would have you; it's the place of optimal living.

You don't have to be anything but what God called you to and that's where you'll be most content. Will God challenge you, and will there be risk in stepping into what He's called you to? Of course. It's just like skipping through the daisies.

A powerful attribute of commissioning encounters is that they most often have symbolic meaning embedded within them. This is often why the Lord does not show up *Himself* every time, or why angels come every time. They'll manifest experiences where they're not *technically* present but it's *from* them still. It's one of the reasons I focus so much on experiences and signs and wonders. Because I've come to learn that His voice sown into these encounters is so profound and makes destiny so easily accessible with great accuracy. It's amazing and often I've seen people skim over the mysteries and keep walking about in a very general way when the specifics are in the mystery.

So often, I'll be in a service talking about encounters, and *boom!* ... people get taken into experiences, and that's what I'm after. And typically, they're unique to the individual's call and manifest so differently across the board.

There's only one time I remember in Colombia, I had foreseen a man's name in a vision in the hotel room before I got there, so I wrote it down in my journal and went looking for Jorge the whole time I was there. I talked about my first experience at a service on this trip, and the anointing opened up for it and this guy got hit. He got smoked.

I found out later from the pastor this guy barely even went to church, and was half backslidden if I remember correctly, and heaven snuck in on him. During a time of praying for the sick, I came up to him and he was acting like he had a taser gun stuck in his ribs; he was just vibrating under the power of God. I prayed for him and he got slammed, laid out, and he was getting hit by power more than anybody I can remember in that service. I wondered what was going on, so he stood back up, still shaking under the power of God, and his face said he didn't know what just happened. He started telling me through my interpreter that right when I was finishing sharing about that encounter, he went into a vision and saw an eagle or a falcon come down and wrap its wings around him, and then he got hit by power.

Thank goodness I brought my journal to church with my Bible. So I asked the interpreter to ask him what his name was, and he told me it was Jorge. When I heard that, I said "Oh, you're the one. Watch this." I opened up my journal, showed him the page where I wrote his name down, and told him heaven already had him pegged. I told him he was the one heaven was looking for. These are the type of things that happen uniquely regarding the nature of your call.

Often, they're different and unique to you for what God's called you to.

REMAINING IN YOUR VEIN

Your greatest reward in heaven is going to be full obedience to Him, not whether you were a prophet, pastor, or apostle. Granted, if you're called to the five-fold, that's awesome. However, those are actually the rarities in Scripture, and they're only called to train up the saints, to be honest with you. The five-fold ministry is to train up the saints to do the work. You still function in your role and work, but you train up others as well. Not to discourage or downplay their role, but I want to encourage you in the other callings that aren't one of the five-fold giftings as well.

Stephen, for example, was a full-out general, and when they picked him he was waiting tables. He wasn't even an apostle or any five-fold gifted minister. He was a modern-day bus boy. Let's look at the context in Acts 6:4. The apostles were sent from Jesus Christ, and eventually they realized they needed to focus and stay faithful in ministry to the Lord and the Word, and they didn't have time to wait on tables. Were they greater than Stephen? No.

I've seen many religious spirits pull from these verses and say, "Tell you what. You go wait tables for a little while and be a servant for a while. Then you can be a part of the greater ministry." They treat these things like Stephen's role was lesser than the apostles' roles. Nobody's better than anybody. What matters is obedience to God in that season.

The early church didn't see it the way we oftentimes do, looking back at this text. Far too often I've seen people try to be sent when they *haven't been sent from above*, and that's why divine encounters are so paramount. Must we have them in order to be sent out for the Gospel? No. But you must experience a commissioning to enter and stay in the vein you're called to. You can't *release* what you don't *carry*.

Stephen was operating in full-out wonders, full of wisdom and boldness and in the power of the Holy Spirit, and he got stoned for the Gospel's sake by Saul. The guy who was picked to wait on tables at the time. He didn't covet a title or a pristine ministry office. He filled his role. As a result, he became the first martyr of the church, and his legacy preaches to us to this day.

We're going to get to heaven one day and Jesus is not going to ask you how well you attained the ministry platforms you thought you needed to occupy. He's going to ask you, "What did you do with what I told you?" Hopefully you'll be able to say what you've done with what you were given one season after another. This is the place where we hear Him say, "Well done, My good and faithful servant."

What God has called you to is specifically between you and Him. It doesn't have to look like a certain or specific thing. How obedient you were to your unique call is what will cause the most fruit to be laid up for you in heaven. There's going to be praying grandmothers that are living in mansions that are far greater than some platform preachers.

It all comes down to obedience. Sometimes we see things from the wrong perspective. Think about the guy that led

Billy Graham to the Lord. He obeyed that day. That fruit goes to his account. Whatever the ornate call is, I want to make sure we obey well in whatever season we're in.

ONE TIME I WAS UP IN WHITEFISH, MONTANA PREACHING, AND I was staying at a pastor's house. We had a three-day conference and on the first night, I was upstairs at the pastor's house with him and a dear friend that I was mentoring at the time and who travelled with me. He was on an air mattress in the room because that was all the extra bedding the pastor had. At about 3 a.m., I had this half-dream, half-encounter where an angel walked into the room up to me from the doorway. I could see him from the waist down and get this: he was wearing construction boots. They represented the workplace, and I could hear the rather loud footsteps on the wood floor as he walked up to my bed.

From what started as a dream, I could see this elevator and a middle-aged woman who had to go up, and I had to release something so it could come back down. In the prophetic part of this dream, it went into this full-out vision of seeing this angel. The elevator was symbolic: going up represented going up to heaven and receiving the call, then coming down to be released and commissioned in it. The angel came, walked right by this guy sleeping on the air mattress, and I smiled because the footsteps were so loud. The angel told me I had to release a commissioning service on the first night of the conference. I thought to myself,

Thank the Lord He sent an angel to tell me that, because I never would have thought to have done that. Everybody knows that we did the fire tunnels on the last night, and spent the other meetings building up toward the *commissioning*.

I'll never forget the next morning when we woke up and my friend on the air mattress told me, "Man, last night was so good. I was sleeping just fine, and right about 3 a.m. all of the sudden I see these lights flashing, and numbers everywhere." He proceeded to tell me he had revelation coming to him as well. In spite of all this, he didn't know that an angel walked right by him at 3 a.m., the fourth watch. His eyes weren't open to see the angel, but he saw the offshoot from that angelic presence. It was lights, numbers, and revelation just from the presence of the angel as he walked by. I told him about the angel I saw come in around the same time.

So we got to the service that night, and I didn't even ask the pastor about this. I've learned you just gotta let it rip and obey heaven. So, we called for a commissioning service and told those present that we were going to commission people into the call of God. During this time, I was laying hands on people, people were getting touched by God, and it was possible some came up just to get prayer. But there was this one lady specifically whom the power of heaven hit.

Sure enough, later I found out that this lady was from out of town and she could only come in for that one service, and she had to leave because she was starting up a new business that the Lord spoke to her about. She needed the anointing and commissioning of God, even in the marketplace. I had picked up on it through the angelic, and even the prophetic dream I had the night before. I saw the call from heaven and the work boots representing marketplace ministry. She was grateful and got hit by the power of God. Only heaven could have known that, but sometimes heaven sets it up divinely like that. God moved the schedule around to reach this one lady who needed a commissioning *that night.*

Sometimes we need the Body of Christ in correlation to trigger the heavenly commission. Some may object and say, "If it's divine, it's got to be sovereign and from the Lord." If that's the case, then why did Paul get hit by a blinding light, and then Jesus spoke to Ananias to go to Paul and pray for him for the scales to fall off his eyes? Heaven still sets it up in such a way that the Body of Christ needs each other, and we've got to hear, flow, and be in sync with heaven. A powerful combustion will happen if we do.

It was awesome to see this lady start a new business in the marketplace, anointed by God. However, the last thing we need her doing is trying to be some evangelist or prophet or something. She's in her handpicked place heaven set her up for, and God only knows the fruit and financial abundance she may be supposed to raise to sow into Kingdom work. She will experience a greater reward than if she had ever tried to take a pulpit or platform ministry or venture into some other sector. Also, let's not forget the people she'll have impact on through her business. Think of it: heaven went out of its way to send an angel to hold a commissioning service for a woman starting a business in the marketplace.

I've seen people who fought and tried to push things for

years because of something they saw or forethought how it was supposed to be. When you do that, you're spinning your wheels. God is patient and longsuffering. Remember, a day with Him is as a thousand years and a thousand years is as a day, so you're not bothering Him one bit. He's not going to change His mind on what you're called to do. You're not going to coax Him into something else. He already had it set up.

He already knows what you're going to do better than you do and knows what's best for the Kingdom and for the full Body moving forward. So it's not like you're going to twist His arm because you'd rather do something else. It doesn't work that way. The quicker we can align to His will and appreciate His fullness, the better. As we do, remember —encounters with Him are not a one-stop shop. Learn to pursue fresh encounters and thereby receive fresh commissionings.

5

COMMISSIONINGS AND CALLINGS

A LOOK AT BIBLICAL SENDINGS

In Genesis 15, we see a commissioning encounter that literally sets up the whole parameter of what Abraham did in his lifetime. I want to share some nuggets that came in the mystery of *how* God approached him. "As the sun was going down, a deep sleep fell on Abram, and behold dreadful and great darkness fell upon him" (Genesis 15:12, ESV).

So instantly we know it's a divine encounter. God is coming to Abram. "Then the Lord said to Abram, 'know for certain that your offspring will be sojourners in a land that is not theirs and will be servants there (basically slaves), they will be afflicted for **400 years**" (Genesis 15:13, ESV, emphasis added). So as we read this you can see why a dreadful darkness fell upon him. It sets the context. It embeds an effect of the Word that's going to be given. The encounters normally have the nature of what God's trying to convey in them.

"They will be afflicted for 400 years. But I will bring judgment on the nation that they serve and afterward they shall come out with great possessions" (Genesis 15:13-14, ESV).

So there's a negative and a positive. Abraham was to lead his people as a father. They're going to go into full-blown slavery, bondage, and confinement for four hundred years, but God also brings the blessing aspect of it to the forefront when He says that He'll bring judgment on the nation they serve. Afterward they shall come out with great possessions, blessing, and be free.

"As for you, you shall go to your fathers in peace and shall be buried in a good old age" (Genesis 15:15, ESV). Isn't that ironic? Many of us would say, "Wait, I'm not signing up for that! I am to father this people that we make into a great name, but most of my waking years are going to be in bondage? And I don't even get to see the riches they come out with?" But that's what Abraham had a grace for. Had he done anything else, it would have been noted by heaven.

"And they shall come back here in the fourth generation, for the iniquity of the Amorites is not yet complete. When the sun had gone down and it was dark, behold, a smoking fire pot and a flaming torch passed between these pieces" (Genesis 15:16-17, ESV). Here we see another mystery in the experience; when the sun had gone down, darkness fell upon him. Verse 12 mentions that the sun was still setting, but now the sun has completely set. In this encounter, it sets up a parameter for quite a dark time to come. God tells Abraham of 400 years of bondage and slavery, but then they'll come out with great possessions, and He'll judge the nation they're surrendered to. Then as we read, the encounter finishes and concludes itself. What leads into this encounter is Abraham sets up sacrifices, and cuts these animals in half like the Lord asks him to, including a three-year old heifer, a three-year old ram, and a turtledove. Abraham doesn't cut the bird in half, but he cuts open the other larger animals as a sacrifice before God. This is where the covenant comes in, because as we know blood makes covenant.

At this point the sun is completely set, it's dark out now, and a smoking firepot and a flaming torch appear and manifest through the pieces of animals that Abraham had cut in half as a sacrifice to God. The text says that on this day the Lord made a covenant with Abraham and further elaborates that He will give him land (see verses 18-21). But that was God's signal, or divine encounter, and it was very mysterious; a smoking pot and a flaming torch manifest. They both appear and start going through the sacrifice Abraham had made to seal the encounter with Him. You look at that and think, *why didn't God just show up and shake his hand or sign something and make a deal?* God is mysterious, and supernatural. Not only that, but these divine encounters contain *calling clues* embedded within them.

If you have had dreams, supernatural encounters, or crazy experiences where God may have taken you out of your body in the past, go back and look at the details of it. Reflect on *why* it took place *then*. Where were you at the time? How did He manifest Himself? Was there a smoking pot and a flaming torch? Did darkness come upon the situation? Did you see light? Did you feel something?

How the manifestation happened is really key. It clues us in on what is to come. It's really important because the two signs God chose to make manifest to Abraham to seal this covenant were the very things his people and offspring were about to go through:

1) The smoking fire pot represents the confinement and the fire being put out, so to speak, of the people. Smoke is produced only when fire is put out. The removal of oxygen smothers the flame, and Abraham's people were going to be like this for 400 years, just like how a pot confines things and removes what the flame needs. It was a picture of the 400 years of slavery to come. That's why the dreadful great darkness came upon him, even in the experience.

2) The flaming torch was the coming alive again, representing *freedom*. A fire in a pot is confined, but a fire on a torch has freedom again. God even mentions in the encounter before He seals it, prophesying that they will come to life again and not just be put out in confinement and slavery and remain smoke. He makes clear that they'll have the freedom to again ignite, grow, and set other things on fire in the will of God.

Since we see in this one encounter alone that speaks profoundly in this mysterious way, it behooves us as people to dissect the nature in which God comes upon us. When we have run-ins with God, there are always *mysteries* tied in. What mysteries tied in with encounters have you experienced? How *have they* and how *are they* pointing to your future and destiny?

In this case, it wasn't a happy, joyful sort of visitation. God was being honest, but He was setting up His people for a *greater* deliverance to come. It was deep and profound. As a result, we can't just look at our encounters and think, *Oh wow, that's pretty cool*. He expresses Himself through mystery that requires us to lean in and seek Him about the meaning. I've come to love wonders and how God speaks in mystery. We need not take it lightly.

MOSES' MYSTERY

"Now Moses was keeping the flock of his father-in-law, Jethro, the priest of Midian, and he led his flock to the west side of the wilderness and came to Horeb, the mountain of God. And the angel of the Lord appeared to him in a flame of fire out of the midst of a bush. He looked, and behold, the bush was burning, yet it was not consumed. And Moses said, 'I will turn aside to see this great sight, why the bush is not burned.' When the Lord saw that he turned aside to see, God called to him out of the bush, 'Moses, Moses!'" (Exodus 3:1-4, ESV).

This is really key. Moses could have looked at it and thought, *that's strange,* and kept walking, but the text says he turned aside and looked again. When God saw that, He called him. That's something I want to encourage you to do; if you even have the slightest inkling God's up to something, *lean into it.* Trust me, that's how I raise my children—to be childlike in faith. I don't care if it's odd, doesn't seem spiritual, or catches you off guard. If you have a divine curiosity—lean into it. Steward it. If you're in a grocery store and you just feel inclined, like God spoke to you about something, you're better off just turning aside, because it may unfold something greater. You don't want to say, "Ah, no. Probably was nothing. I'll just keep walking."

Prior to this event with Moses, it says he was tending the flock of his father-in-law Jethro, the priest of Midian, and led the flock to the west side of the wilderness. That's interesting. So this means the encounter happened where? In the wilderness. Where did Moses' whole call revolve around as we read on later? The wilderness. So in the wilderness he came to Horeb, the mountain of God, and here the angel of the Lord appeared to him. How? In a flame of fire out of the midst of a bush.

There are all sorts of manners of manifestations God can come in, but in this instance, He came in a fire, in a bush, in the wilderness. A fire does two things. First, a fire in Scripture purges things. It separates and purifies. When gold is put through the heat, the impure is separated from the pure. Scripture tells of how we need to be refined by fire.

Secondly, according to Scripture, fire is often in tandem with God's jealousy for His people, "For the Lord your God is a consuming fire, a jealous God" (Deut 4:24). Hebrews 12:25-29 says, "See that you do not refuse him who is speaking. For if they did not escape when they refused him who warned them on earth, much less will we escape if we reject him who warns from heaven. At that time his voice shook the earth, but now he has promised, 'Yet once more and I will shake not only the earth, but also the heavens.'"

This phrase, "yet once more," indicates the removal of things that are shaken—that is, things that have been made—in order that the things that cannot be shaken may remain. The Word goes on to say, "Therefore let us be grateful for receiving a kingdom that cannot be shaken, and thus let us offer to God acceptable worship with reverence and awe, for our God is a consuming fire." So again, as this passage in the New Testament elaborates, the fire is a purifying thing. But also, it speaks of His jealousy.

In this context, we know Moses' commission. Yet we also are clued into the details and settings of his commission. He encounters fire in the wilderness. Fire that purges and is jealousy burning in God for His people. Moses then proceeds to spend much of his life in the wilderness, amidst his people who are being purged by fire in preparation for Joshua to lead them into the Promised Land. Essentially all of Moses's journey and major role of his call was in the application of God as fire, separating and purging of his people not only from Pharaoh, but their very heart, in order to lead them to a greater place.

It's very easy to look at this one encounter and you think, *Wow, a burning bush. That's pretty incredible, and God spoke out of it; that's great.* But no, God came in the very nature of what Moses' whole call was going to be: a purging fire in the wilderness. It's symbolism pointing directly to destiny.

JOSHUA'S JOURNEY

JOSHUA HAD AN ENCOUNTER WITH THE ANGEL OF THE LORD OF hosts where he basically gets the baton handed to him to lead the people through the Jordan and into the Promised Land. As soon as their feet hit the Promised Land, the circumcision and Passover were complete. The Bible says they ate of the land and the manna ceased the very next day. That right there was the *true shift*. They had been fed supernaturally under Moses daily and they even got into the Promised Land, but had to go through *Passover* and eat of the land. As soon as they did, they became part of that new commission and land.

Joshua was Moses' predecessor, and experienced many things previously, but like we've already established, there's installments to these encounters. Joshua was no longer living under the installment that Moses brought forth. Something new was about to happen. We see in Joshua 5:13, Joshua has his own commissioning encounter.

"When Joshua was by Jericho, he lifted up his eyes and looked, and behold, a man was standing before him with his drawn sword in his hand. And Joshua went to him and said to him, 'Are you for us, or for our adversaries?' And he said, 'No; but I am the commander of the army of the Lord. Now I have come.' And Joshua fell on his face to the earth and worshiped and said to him, 'What does my lord say to his servant?' And the commander of the Lord's army said to Joshua, 'Take off your sandals from your feet, for the place where you are

Commissionings and Callings | 57

standing is holy.' And Joshua did so" (Joshua 5:13-15, ESV).

His encounter was not near a burning bush and had nothing to do with fire. Instead, it was an angel of the Lord of hosts with a drawn sword. Why? Because Joshua's destiny and calling were different than Moses'. Joshua's wasn't about purging fire, but it was about something else. What was *his* about? Conquest and battle. He spent most of his life conquering and battling in the land of Canaan, driving out enemy forces. This is why the angel had a drawn sword. Again, we see the encounter projecting elements of the future call of God.

I'M REMINDED OF A TIME WHEN AN ANGEL CAME TO ME IN THE night, first in a dream. This wasn't a commissioning encounter, but it really helped with understanding. The kindest man you would have ever known came to me in this dream, the type who would give you the shirt off his back and do anything he could to assist. All of the sudden the dream slipped into a night vision where my spiritual eyes were open to the actual angel, nine feet tall, standing at the foot of my bed. His head went up into the recess of my ceiling, full, white wings wrapped around that looked like 400 pounds of straight muscle. It was very sobering when you saw him glorified, but right before that in the dream I was glad he told me his name, and that he was one of my angels. The meaning of his name meant to usurp, which means overtake or take the place of by force, supplant, and overthrow, which is really key.

Even if God sends an angel and a name is given, you want to dissect the meaning of it all. In this case the meaning of the angel's name, to usurp, is basically what Joshua was doing; to take the place of by force, supplant, overthrow, unseat, dethrone. That's what Joshua and the Israelites came in to do. A Promised Land-type of commission; you come in to dethrone Jericho and take the spoils. It's a very apostolic, building type of mantle.

There's so much in encounters when you experience them. It's not just an interesting encounter shrouded in mystery that can't be solved. No, it reflects your future and is able to be dissected, understood, and discovered.

ADDITIONAL EPIPHANIES

We all know the story of Paul on the road to Damascus, and we've covered it in this book. We know this blinding light came and caused what looked to be scales upon Paul's eyes; but then God called Ananias to come to him, and when he prayed for him, those scales fell off. Paul was called to a blinded people to bring the true light and revelation of God, that scales may fall from their eyes, just as what had happened to him in his commissioning experience. Again, the nature of Paul's call was embedded in his experience itself, as he would go about opening the eyes of gentiles who previously were blinded to covenant with God.

Look at Isaiah's initiation in the sixth chapter of Isaiah,

for another example. A burning coal touches the mouth of a prophet. The people of God needed cleansing and purification. Isaiah is touched with a purifying coal to preach a purifying message. See, all of these encounters are intentionally crafted by God. There's nothing wasted and nothing out of place.

When you look at prophets of old like Ezekiel, Daniel, and others, you find they would often preface their prophecies with the date, the time of year, and even the place that they happened. They were so intentional about recording the *when*, *where*, and often the *why*. They had an understanding that encounters with God were wrapped up in meaning and symbolism that they couldn't afford to miss.

We could continue going all over Scripture and dissecting more examples of people's commissioning encounters, but the examples above ought to solidify our hearts in the intentional design of God encounters. Don't overlook the symbolism, context, and meaning of these events. How, when, and where God encounters you is really profound, and it will help you understand why you have a grace to walk in certain areas and not so much in others. When you start to really hone in and see your call clearly, you understand why it's no wonder you don't have a passion or an interest in certain things like others do, but something else comes so easy and natural for you and doors are opened up over and over again. It's the enlightenment of the encounter and not just the encounter itself that produces long-term fruit in our lives and destinies.

6

SURPRISES AND SUDDENLIES

THE UNPREDICTABLE NATURE OF ENCOUNTERS

Thank God that He didn't leave us alone in the midst of the earth while He ascended on high. We haven't been left hanging. He sent the Holy Ghost. You can see that from day one He loves to be involved in the affairs of His people. It was *always* and *only* on our end that we brought separation.

There are so many different facets to God and His Kingdom, and it's all so beautiful because it points back to His voice. All of it, whether it be signs and wonders, the angelic realm, Jesus Christ Himself, the Holy Ghost, the Father, the Ancient of Days—it's all Him. We need it all because Jesus needed it all in His earthly ministry. I've really come to appreciate all of it because it's all Him, and I've come to learn that I don't really have the answers to what I might need, so I just need Him. He is above *answers* in my life. And I don't care how He wants to show up, just bring it, Jesus!

We are not just talking about this to talk about it, but we're talking about it for the experience of the very thing to come upon us. We want Jesus. That's what this whole thing's about; to stir up atmosphere, impartation, and encounter with Him that we may love Him and know Him and walk away with Him more intimately and in union and oneness with His presence, His voice, and His likeness that we reflect on the earth.

Like we mentioned earlier, divine means *of or from God*. We've seen that He's got many different facets and means by which He shows up. It's well documented in the entire canon of Scripture. There are a few additional run-ins with man involving flames and the angelic that I want to highlight. All of them have a common denominator.

- Tongues of fire and mighty rushing wind (Acts 2).
- Daniel, one of the most profound prophets of old, meets Gabriel (archangel) (Daniel 10).
- Moses encounters the burning bush, which was the voice of God, and if you read closely, it was an angel of the Lord. The Scriptures say an angel spoke out of the burning bush (see Exodus 3:3).
- Angels are called God's messengers, flames, and winds of fire—sometimes they can appear as the very substance themselves (Hebrews 1:7).

What is the common denominator? It's not just flames and the angelic. It's the fact that these saints didn't predict how or when the encounter would take place. It's one thing to have a zeal for God, but in your zeal, don't start thinking that you've got God figured out. If we have a preconceived mindset on how God's going to encounter us, then about 99.9 percent of the time it will be different than that. What happens is that you can miss what God is trying to do in any given moment because you get tunnel vision on a way He's "supposed" to meet with you.

Don't get me wrong, I'm all about hunger and tenacity and I believe that God is a rewarder of those who diligently seek Him. I take purposefully the things of heaven and pursue them. I hit them like a piñata and break them down and tear the veils with hunger and pursuit. God is okay with asking, seeking, knocking. It's just that the way we're wired, we have these preconceived ways of how we want God to encounter us. We begin to think it's going to be this certain way. I'm just telling you, quite often, and even most often, the way He encounters you isn't the way you thought it would be. Be single-minded in your pursuit of God, but don't be single-minded in your expectation of how He will show up.

Look at Acts 2, for example, the first time the Holy Ghost hit the earth. Jesus said, "Just wait until you've been endued with power from on high." They had no clue what this was going to look like. The 120 were in the upper room and just obeyed the pursuit in diligence. But it happened in a *suddenly* manner. Nowhere before did anyone have a clue about how and where it was going to happen. Typically if it had been penned in the Old Testament, it was in such a parabolic way that was not literal. They wouldn't have known because of the cryptic nature of Old Covenant prophecy.

A literal and sudden sound of a rushing, mighty wind blew through, and what appeared to be tongues of fire came and rested upon their heads. Check it out in the context of what we're talking about regarding divine encounters. They had no clue what would happen. We often think we do, but the longer I'm in this thing and the more I spend time with Jesus, and know Him, the more I realize I have zero clue at all. You gain a lot of insight and knowledge in the complexity of who He is, and you see how really simple the foundation of it all is set up. A better way to put it, is that another layer gets pulled back and you see that there's still a million layers beneath.

With Moses, it was a burning bush, and such an encounter never came again, before or after. It caught him by surprise. Joshua was probably expecting a burning bush or something because his leader had that, but instead the angel of the Lord of hosts appeared to him.

Daniel saw Gabriel on the bank of the Nile. John was caught up. Thomas felt Christ's side. Stephen saw open heavens. God is so vast and creative. Even with every encounter, He'll mimic aspects of some encounters to you that you've seen in the Bible before, but only to give you clues. But typically, you never see repeated encounters because He's so creative and ever so personal. Why is a handwritten letter more impactful than giving someone a Hallmark card with someone else's writing? One is personal;

the other has been duplicated and commercialized over and over.

God is so personal and wants to hit you from many angles. It's better to clear the slate and not have forethought to the way God's going to encounter you because you could get so tunnel-visioned that you miss certain things.

You may be thinking, *well if it's God, it's supernatural, and surely I am not going to miss it.* Moses was walking by the bush while it was burning, and it says he *looked again.* He could have kept walking and thought to himself, *Hmm, that's interesting. The sun must have come through at just the right angle. After all, it's been a dry season.* But the Scripture says he looked and leaned in, so as to see.

Jesus was walking on the water (see the gospel of Matthew, chapter 14), as though He was going to walk by them, but the disciples called out to Him. When He appeared hidden after the resurrection when a few disciples were walking on the road to Emmaus, it says their hearts were burning within them. He masked Himself in a way where they didn't know who He was, and He was going to keep walking by, but they urged Him to stay with them.

What I'm getting at with these examples is that we can have tunnel vision and miss windows and seasons of opportunity. It's better to clear the slate and posture ourselves before God in a way where we don't have a clue what to expect, but we cry out to God, "Lord, just come! I don't care *how* You want to come, but I'll take it all! Whenever, however, daily—I don't care. Just come. I'm hungry. Please touch me. Please come. I don't care.

Cloud of witnesses, or Jesus Christ Himself, the angelic, the Ancient of Days!" When you open yourself like this, the Lord often gives you something you don't *expect* because it's something you didn't know that you *needed*. Why? Because it's something you'll need for the next season in front of you.

7
COVENANT AND CONTINGENCIES
OBEYING THE HEAVENLY VISION

Here's a key to making the most of encounters. They're not just so we can say *wow* and tell a friend how amazing it was. Encounters aren't for mere entertainment. If God's going out of His way to have a run-in with you in the earth, there's so much weight on it for years to come, no matter how minute it seems. This goes back to His nature. He's so relational, and so loving that when He shows up on the scene, He's so infatuated with you and loves you that He's not only coming in love, but the nature of who He is. He's always speaking in the experiences.

The Bible says, "His word cannot return void" (Isaiah 55:11). Of course, the *logos* Word of God, but also *rhema*. He is *both/and*. God is never *either/or* in this context, of course. In every experience, try Him. Read throughout Scripture. He never encounters mankind without a speaking. Even if it's visionary—it's still Him speaking.

The Bible describes Him as a *covenant* God. He's not just trying to experience you for a *wow* moment of affection. Although He is, it just doesn't stop there because He's so deeply infatuated and in love with you. He also cares about His call on you way more than you do. He is ever so interested in your destiny being fulfilled because He knows that's where you'll be most happy and find the most fulfillment. It's where you'll most reflect His glory. It's a reciprocal, glorious thing. Remember, encounters with Him are covenants He's making with you.

The Bible says God is not a man that He should lie. Like I mentioned a moment ago, the Scripture says God's Word will not return void. Men and women change. I've run with a bunch and see a lot come and go. Let's just be honest; you can't often put a lot of weight on people. God-filled people, sure, you can trust and run with them on a covenant level, but even then, never as much as God. Anything God ever tells you is concrete, permanent, and eternal, filled with covenant and promise that you can always take to the bank and hang your hat on, for that matter. Whereas, if we're honest, with mankind, they change in seasons. Motives and things shift, and I'm not trying to talk about how bad mankind is, but the Bible says that God by comparison is not a man *that He can lie* or do things mankind is *comfortable doing*.

Why am I emphasizing covenant promise and the integrity of God's Word to us so much? Because I don't care how old the encounter is, what God said stands true to this day. If He said it, He meant it, and it never will change. I've just seen too many people that I've personally run with fall away. I mean people who were infatuated with Jesus, would fast, pray, knew the Lord, and had real-deal encounters with Him. Typically it starts at a slow leak ... a lack of time in the secret place. It causes men to fall away. I've seen it. I've seen men who fell off and came back, and others who have fallen off for good as of this writing. Oftentimes they don't realize that call, and that the covenant promise of God remain, but it usually starts with neglecting the secret place and falling off and aborting the call. With any given experience with God, you can take it to the bank as a covenant and promise that's made with you. If it's not seen as a covenant promise, you'll treat it like a flimsy promise from man and it won't have the impact that it should on your life.

Also, every encounter from Him is ultimately Him speaking to you, and an endowment of some part of your destiny. In every experience, the point is not so we can *feel* the glory or experience some profound sensation. Every time He shows up it's with deep meaning, with the deepest eternal love you've ever known, because He *is* love. He's not merely a loving Person, He is the Person who *is* love. When He shows up, His encounter to you is sealed with the promise of His steadfast nature and unchanging, blissful disposition toward your life.

I was just talking to my mother yesterday, whom I love dearly, and she told me of a profound and prophetic dream she had and called me about it. I was helping interpret the dream for her. She had been seeking the Lord at morning and night, which can be dangerous (in a good way) when you're seeking God at night, because as she learned, your dream life becomes more crystal clear. You go to sleep with your spiritual antenna tuned in to the Spirit, and the soulish things like the weeds of the day and mind, rhythm, and emotions are pulled out. So, as a result, these powerful dreams have been coming to her recently. One of the things we were talking about in the conversation was how God's voice in any given season is the thing you hang onto. God's presence, which is where His voice comes out of (of course, you've got to get close enough to hear Him), but God's voice to you in any given season is always what you bank everything on. You hinge your whole life off of what He's saying.

So I've learned, and I'm trying to learn this better in life. To hang on to what God has said and nothing else. I get it, you're busy, you have trials, tribulations. There are so many opinions and decisions to make and lots going on emotionally, along with desires and open doors, shut doors, etc. For me, I don't even go off on any of that anymore as best as I can. I try to detach from all of life, even my soulish desires, if you will, and simply cling to the voice and will of God. "Not my will, Your will be done Lord," ought to be the posture of our hearts. From the place of detachment from the world and attachment to God, the encounters are worth taking to the bank and eating from for many, many years to come.

LOOKING WHERE HE LOOKS

It's so crucial we learn to hear His voice more clearly than ever. Doors will open up, and sometimes they seem so obviously from God, but in fact it's the enemy trying to get you ahead of schedule, when in actuality you'll be behind schedule because doing this thing will make you wind up going around more mountains. I've had some major doors open up that a lot of people wouldn't have even hesitated to go through. They might think, *that's got to be the acceleration and favor of the Lord.* Yet, I held it before the Lord, and it became clear it wasn't His will. His voice is what you hang on to in any season, and it's always embedded into the encounters and experiences.

You're going to have emotional highs and lows, doors of favor, and doors that close. Seasons of peace and seasons of war. I've learned to not even pay attention anymore to the news and what's happening in the natural, but I just look for the news lines of heaven and what God's voice is saying to me. When He's highlighting an issue, then I'm focusing on it. If He is concerned, I get concerned. If He's speaking a certain direction, I'm following it. I don't really ask anymore because He knows. We just need to say, "When, where, and how high to jump?" We don't do this with a slave mentality, although the Scripture does tell us we're bondservants, but I'm talking about a place of infatuation and trust.

As I continue to hammer on the trustworthy, covenant nature of encounters—don't miss that obedience is key. God's love is *always unconditional,* but God's covenant promises to you are *extremely conditional.*

A lot of people don't like this teaching a whole lot, and to be honest with you, it's not my favorite either, but it's the truth. And truth sets us free. God's love to us is unconditional. I tell my kids the same thing. It doesn't matter what they do, they know I love them. Yet His promises and experiencing fullness is dependent upon obedience. Paul himself spoke about encountering Christ and said, "I was not disobedient to the heavenly vision" (Acts 26:19). This means that obedience is integral to the system.

You may be thinking, *Well, Brian, if God spoke it, surely it will come to pass, wouldn't it? After all, you just said His Word shall not return to Him void. And God's sovereign. If He spoke it, it will come forth.* But that's not biblical. Again, it sounds good, and I wish it were the case probably more than you, but it's simply not. His love for you will never change. The Bible says Jesus Christ was crucified before the foundations of the earth. This whole plot was planned from start to finish way before creation even occurred. Jesus, to this day, is in heaven with holes in His hands for all of us. But the access point of the fullness of these promises is highly hinged upon obedience. Don't get me wrong; God's sovereign, I get it. The divinity of God and what He can do is an impressive reality, yet He gave man a *will*. Our obedience can speed up or delay promises from their fulfillment and make them not even applicable in our lives.

"If you faithfully obey the commands I'm giving you this day, I'll send rain on your land in its season, both autumn and spring rain, so that you may gather in your grain new wine and olive oil. I'll provide grass in the fields for your cattle, and you'll eat and be satisfied" (Deuteronomy 11:13-15).

"If you fully obey the Lord your God and carefully follow all the commands I give you today, the Lord your God will set you high above all the nations of the earth. All these blessings will come on you and accompany you if you obey the Lord your God" (Deuteronomy 28:1-2).

All throughout chapter 28 of Deuteronomy, you'll see numerous "ifs" in there. His covenant with us contains a massive contingency called *obedience*. He didn't want robots and drones. He wants people that love Him by their own free will.

One might say, *Well, that's Old Testament, brother. Things have changed since the blood of Jesus. I'm under the New Testament.* Jesus was crucified before the foundations of the earth (Revelation 13:8). The Old Covenant is still the nature of God, and never changed, since God is the same yesterday, today, and forever. The Old Covenant is a reflection or shadow of the *real thing*. The access point by which we can be saved changed drastically in the New Covenant through the blood of Jesus. But the nature of God never changed.

Again, the crucifixion and resurrection of Jesus Christ was foreshadowed before the foundation of the world, so really it was the master plan of God leading up to it in a natural timeline, so we could say, "Oh, *this* is *that*." But on the eternal side before heaven, it had already happened. It was preplanned. All that being said, God's nature has never changed. His love is unconditional; His promises *are* conditional. Old to New Testament, none of that changes. What changes drastically is the *access point* by grace through faith are we saved, and not through bulls and goats and such things under the Old Testament.

Matthew 24:13 says, "But the one who stands firm to the

end shall be saved." That's *conditional*. Another example would be, *"If* you keep my commands, you will remain in my love, just as I have kept my father's commands and remain in his love" (John 15:10). It's all so very conditional. Just because you had an encounter doesn't mean you'll eat the fruit of it forever. The Word given in that moment of glory must be obeyed and carried out. Begin to see your encounters as covenants with contingencies. Take note of the encounters of old that you've experienced and see about obeying them in a fresh way. In so doing, you'll experience the drastic benefit of obedience to the heavenly vision, so to speak.

8

CONTENTION AND CONFLICT
THE ENCOUNTER BEFORE THE STORM

Often, the depth of the encounter you have reflects the amount of opposition you will face in seeing the promise in that encounter come to fruition. The greater the encounter, the greater the opposition that follows. The more profound the *experience*, the more profound the *resistance*. I should say, not exclusively, but definitely inclusive and highly likely, at least in my personal life and my understanding of the Scripture. The more profound the experience, not all the time but more often than not, the more profound the resistance. The more memorable the visitation, the more pronounced the contention to see that very thing come to pass. This is often why God allows the experience to be so profound. It's not the only reason, but it's is one of the reasons. I know for my own life I've often looked back and said, "Thank God He did it this way, because, boy, if I knew what was coming after..." Again, it's not the only reason, but it's a *major* one.

Again, God is so multifaceted, calculated, and perfect in all that He does. But I need to be honest with you because I'd be misleading you by getting you stirred up with hunger, just get you excited for burning-bush experiences but leave you unprepared for certain challenging seasons that follow. I don't want you to think, *wait a minute, nobody told me it would be like this.* Moses had challenges with Pharaoh and the Israelites after the burning bush. Joshua had plenty of battles after the impartation. Paul faced nasty persecution after the Damascus encounter. Challenges follow encounters quite often.

See, He knows you will need something very firm, concrete, and pronounced to hold on to with what all that's coming ahead. In the midst of the journey, the trials, and the time of building character you'll need an experience to draw from. The opposition from the enemy will sidetrack you or get you to abort the entire plan if you forget the experiences of times past. The enemy does this with many. It's the reason why God was so adamant about recording the testimony of the Lord. For if we remember it, we can duplicate it. It will give us *staying power.*

The voice of the Lord during an encounter with Him is the lighthouse in the middle of the storm you always focus on. I can't tell you how many times I go back to memories of experiencing God—it's like the plumb line of life. So never forget this: your experiences and encounters that have His voice in them are the plumb line that you follow and gauge everything against. It is the crosshairs of life, so to speak, everything goes *through* it.

If we're honest with ourselves, life just throws everything it's got at us—people, the enemy, and everything else—but all that is neither here nor there anymore as you begin to learn what the Father's voice is saying. By camping out there, you dismiss the cares of this life and you thwart the attempts of the enemy. You put all your eggs in that one basket, and if you're a gambler, you're *betting everything on His voice*. Experiences are this way, and they get you through. I can think back on how many times in my own life I thank God for the encounters because I didn't know what was soon coming.

You can weather the storm because you have that profound peace, and you're able to go back to what God said and declare, "No, I remember that encounter, that experience, and it was undeniable." It's why He makes it so substantial, profound, and memorable.

I truly want to *establish* this because it will help many of you reading this who've had experiences before. Perhaps even as you're reading this, the Lord is reminding you of encounters from the past. God will remind you of what He said before you got thrown off into the wilderness for several years. Trust me, I've been there. A lot of people see me and others now and don't know about the journey we took to get here.

The enemy tries to steal, kill, and destroy, but Jesus has come that we may have life and more abundantly (see John 10:10). Oh how often the enemy comes with doubt and circumstances that look the opposite of what God told you.

Yet these things ought not move you since you've already been moved by *promise* and not the problem.

The Scriptures record in Matthew 3 and Luke 3 the events that took place just before Christ was sent into the wilderness. Jesus is the highest standard of all things. Jesus was 100 percent man as well as 100 percent God, and in these parallel passages we see God having an encounter with the Spirit right before going out in the wilderness and being tested for forty days.

The heavens were opened, and the Holy Spirit descended on Jesus in bodily form like a dove. If you read that really slowly, you'll notice it says the Holy Spirit descended *like a dove*. I know a lot of people and perhaps old movies show the Holy Spirit coming down this way as a literal dove. The text doesn't say that. It says the heavens opened, first off. Which is crazy enough. Then the Holy Spirit descended upon Jesus in *bodily* form. I would love to see what that looked like through encounter experience because as the text says, it was *like* a dove. We see this even in the book of Revelation when John sees the four living creatures he says are *like* a lion, or had a face *like* a man, *like* an ox, or an eagle in flight. Those things are not what they *really* were, but *like* them.

I have had a few heavenly encounters, and there are certain things you'll see and it's as if your mind is trying to compute and bounce it off of stuff you know from the natural realm here. The best thing you can do is describe it as being *like* something familiar. The apostle Paul said there were things he saw he couldn't even mention, colors and objects on that side which were unable to be communicated with early descriptions.

Again, the heavens opened, the Holy Spirit descended upon Jesus in bodily form *like* a dove. You can just imagine the tenderness, or the delicacy of a dove descending. Then, there was an audible voice, to boot. I mean, the heavens open, the Holy Spirit in bodily form descends, an audible voice is heard—this is a full-out encounter!

I figure if Jesus needed encounters, how much more do we? The angels came to Him twice, as did the witnesses on the Mount of Transfiguration. Jesus is the role model by which all things go by. In Jesus' earthly ministry, He had the Holy Spirit descend on Him, which we know transpired again in Acts 2, as He *also* fell on the disciples. If Jesus *needed* all these encounters and commissioned His disciples to experience them, then so be it, that's the *standard*. That's our aim as well. Not only that, but as far as miracles are concerned, He says in the Word that we'll do greater works. Not lesser works.

The audible voice of the Father said, "This is my Son, with whom I am well pleased" (Matthew 3:17). What took place after the descending, the voice, and the open heavens? He was led by the Spirit that came upon Him into the wilderness. Mark's version says He was amongst wild beasts, and came against the greatest opposition any man on this side of heaven could, satan himself. That was no small battle. This is not the prince of Persia or the prince of Greece from the Old Testament anymore. This is Lucifer himself. It's not a demon or a regional principality, this is satan himself.

This isn't to give glory to the dark side, or to honor the demonic hierarchy, but Ephesians 6 is clear that we wrestle not against flesh and blood.

I don't give a lot of credit or focus upon the enemy; I focus on Jesus. Why? Because intimacy is the *highest point* of warfare. You ascend above these things with intimacy. But if we're real about it, we face opposition. I've had some very real demonic battles, and so did Jesus. So, Christ, being the standard, battled darkness. So why do we think we're not susceptible to running into these things also? Honestly, I get a little nervous around people who never have opposition. That's not to say you should feel bad if you haven't or that you should go running and looking around for devils. However, when you walk with the Spirit long enough, warfare will ensue. Notice though, Christ's powerful encounter was the prerequisite for harsh battle. Likewise, friends, your open-heaven moment can often be followed by warfare. The Lord kindly preps us for the fight with irreversible experiences with Him.

I could tell you story after story of profound encounters I've had that were followed by hellacious seasons of warfare, trials, tribulations, testing, character building, and seemingly deserts or wildernesses that then always lead to greater *authority* and *power*. That's always the trump card of God. He always does it. The quicker we can learn this, the better we can get through these seasons.

He'll put Goliaths up against you so you can take them out to give Him glory. He'll tell Gideon to cut his army down to three hundred by having them drink out of the water to separate them so that He can be glorified by delivering them out of the hand of the enemy (see Judges 7). He'll put you in situations where the battle's real to take you into a greater authority. The end result is absolutely a greater measure of authority and power. The Bible says Jesus came out of the wilderness in the power of the Spirit. Then, obviously, all heaven broke loose with dead raisings, food multiplications, disciples gathered, blind eyes opened, walking on water, you name it. *This* is where it all begins.

Again, if one of Jesus' most profound experiences was followed up by a head-to-head with the enemy, don't be surprised if you see the same. I've just seen it too many times. I remember the spirit of death came once. It was day thirty-eight of a forty-day fast, and it was realer than real. On this occasion, I was rushed to the emergency room. I've experienced all kinds of attacks over the years. I don't talk about them a lot, but the dark side is real, and it's going to check you out. But if you stand firm like Ephesians 6 says, you come out with greater authority.

A few years back, I remember I would stand up behind pulpits and just try and do an intro and say, "I'm so glad to be here." I would start weeping, and heaven would come in, and I could feel a sense of vibration behind me. Shortly afterward I was rushed to the ER and lost about ten pounds in nine days. I just want to encourage you, as you face these things, there's always God's trump card waiting to give you greater authority and take you further into Him.

PAUL'S PREREQUISITE

As Acts 9 records, Saul was on the road to Damascus when a blinding light encounter with an audible voice from Jesus took place. This was followed by fourteen years of ongoing preparation in the wilderness (read Galatians 2:1). It's easy to read Galatians fast and miss that, but the one quick verse indicates that before everything Paul did, he was in preparation for fourteen years. Obviously, Paul wrote about two-thirds of the New Testament, and we are well aware of all the persecution he went through. It was a hard road for Paul in many ways. Yet consider the encounter which prepped him for all of these things. It was so profound; a bright light, an audible voice, blind eyes, and more.

In Acts 9, God speaks in a vision to Ananias, "Go to Saul. I must tell him all he must suffer for my name's sake as he's called to the Gentiles" (Acts 9:16). This moment marked Paul in an awesome manor. Sure enough, at the end of the book of Acts, years and years later—he is getting locked up before King Agrippa. He stands up and says, "Oh King, this day I was coming down on the road to Damascus and a blinding light came down out of heaven" (Acts 22:6). He could recall it so fresh after many years had passed. It was such a landmark transition in his life. He had it to hold on to through all the floggings, the prison time, the persecutions, and he knew the call. The circumstances he faced never got him off his path.

Stay close to Jesus in the secret place. I've seen people with profound encounters get off who didn't stay intimate with Jesus. That's the crux of things: intimacy with God. But from there, these encounters and landmarks are things you can always go back to and say, "No, I am called to the Gentiles, even though I'm facing such persecution and being locked up," like Paul did with his calling.

Even our spouses sometimes may say, "Yeah, well, what about this?" Our response? "Okay, that's fine, but what did God's voice say?" Husbands, wives, close friends, ministers, or others may say things to get you off track. They might not even have bad intentions in any way. Yet it all comes back to, *what did God say?* When you revert back to the voice of God from that encounter, it will make concrete your calling and keep you from falling.

ABRAHAM'S VISITATION

Abraham had numerous run-ins with God, including new covenants being formed with God and promises made to be fulfilled through future generations. Yet we'll focus on one particular visitation in this text. He was traveling on the initial word of the Lord to get out of his home country and across Canaan. The Lord told him to leave his father's house and country and go to a place where God would make a great nation out of his descendants (see Genesis 12:1). He leaves without knowing exactly where he is going, but if we read the account closely, it states he went through Canaan. When he crosses this land, the Lord appears to him and says, "To your offspring, I'll give this land" (Genesis 12:7). Abraham keeps going. Ever noticed that? Why not camp out there if God said He's going to give it to him? He didn't have offspring yet. Interestingly, he crossed a region that God was going to give to him.

Don't ever forget those encounters, because as you're going to see, you'll have a lot of opposition going back to them. Oftentimes you'll have character building or the enemy testing you. We see it over and over in Scripture, and if we just obey and follow, then we'll come through and make it in the end. Sure, we can delay seasons longer than they need to be. If that's the case and you delayed it, *why cry about it?* Let's go on. Jesus has got our best interest at hand.

Abraham obviously doesn't have any offspring at this point when he has the encounter, but that's what they're for —to hang on to. God is not a man that He can lie. Abraham keeps going straight into a famine, and then to Egypt, where the risk of losing his wife is a real possibility. So at this point, Abraham's plotting and planning now to get through, and has Sarah tell them she's his sister. They go through Egypt only to come full circle.

After the encounter, he experiences a famine and almost loses his life and wife. Can you imagine the doubt he must have battled toward the promise of God? I don't know why God set it up this way, but He arranged it, so these things often follow the encounter. The very thing you just experienced and encountered, the more profound it is, that very thing will be challenged tremendously. You've got to hang on to it. But it comes full circle, and we read in chapter 13 of Genesis that God appears to Ahimelech and he gives Abraham all kinds of cattle. In other words, they increase and come back to Canaan with more possessions than when they left.

It's always going to turn out in your favor, but sometimes if we're not there yet, we start to doubt. We can get off focus and get into disobedience and focus on the delay. We've got to obey. Learn to *obey* in the midst of *delay*. We come back full circle in the story, and you see God's voice come to fruition like He said. They camp out in Canaan and eventually have Isaac and the promise is fulfilled. Yet remember, trial followed the encounter. Opposing circumstances tried to prove God a liar, yet God just proved the circumstances a liar and He, Himself, to be true.

Here are a couple more experiences involving prerequisite encounters from the Word. At the burning bush, Moses was given two signs: a leprous hand and his staff turned into a snake. This profound encounter at the burning bush followed by continual battling with Pharaoh, making even his own people mad at him because of the resistance Pharaoh put on the people of Israel. Moses was just trying to obey the Lord, and he had his burning-bush experience to go back to in order to keep himself centered on what God had told him to do. These are keys to dissolving discouragement in your life.

Look at King David in 1 Samuel 16. He was sought out and found by one of the most profound prophets of God in not only that day and era, but in *all of history*. The prophet Samuel pours a horn of oil over his head to anoint him king of all Israel, followed by the Spirit rushing upon him. After this, David entered a season of fleeing for his life from Saul, hiding in caves in foreign lands, now having to pretend he's a madman with saliva running down his beard to protect his life. He marked gates so the kings of these foreign lands wouldn't capture and kill him (see 1 Samuel 21). Yet the oil on his head and that encounter with Saul, I believe, gave him *staying power* to continue to push for God's promise to come to pass.

I want to close this chapter with this. God allows the experience to be so profound and memorable and substantial in our life to hold us during times of trial, but also simply because *it's who He is*. He loves to manifest and let His glory hit the temple so strongly you can't even stand to minister. He loves to manifest a pillar of cloud by day and a pillar of fire by night to lead the people out.

Look at the crazy, manifested wonders on display for Pharaoh or Jesus multiplying food and walking on water. He loves to have these landmark moments; these pockets and these windows of experiencing you, interrupting your world in order to make it memorable. He's an experiential and *encountering* God. He *can't not* be. This is all part of His personality; He can't not be Himself. Oh how He sits on the edge of heaven, longing to encounter a people who know the Kingdom of heaven is at hand.

9

METHODS AND MODELS
THE VARYING MEANS OF ENCOUNTER

Typically, but not exclusively, encounters come *from or of* the Father, *from or of* the Son Jesus, *from or of* the Holy Spirit, *from or of* angelic beings, *from or of* the cloud of witnesses. Are these the only places they can come from? By no means. In Scripture we have the living creatures, the watcher angels from different levels (see Daniel 4). Obviously for it to be a divine encounter, it's got to come from the divine realm, which is *supernatural*. The cloud of witnesses is distinct from angels, and the Father is distinct from the Son, obviously. It can get quite complex on the other side, but the base foundation to keep in mind is that these divine encounters originate in God. For example, if I wanted to get a message to you—I could tell you myself, I could send friend A, I could send friend B, or I could send friend C. Whether it's myself, or friend A, B, or C—it's still originating in me. Don't think that an encounter with the angelic is somehow separate from the Father. No, these things originate in the Father.

I say "of or from" because each divine authority from whichever heavenly order I just mentioned can fully orchestrate a divine encounter involving you and not appear to be *technically* present, or not need to be the focal point of the divine experience. You can have an encounter *of* the Father, and He is there, and you're in an experience with Him, or *from* the Father that was more sown in by revelation and mystery.

See, biblical stories are still alive because the book is alive. It's the *living* Word. Allow me to encourage you as you read the Bible, every time, as best as you can, try to not read it from a habitual posture. Reading out of habit will nullify its power. It's an experiential book, and you want this thing to come out and take you over.

In Hebrews 12, it says we are surrounded by a great cloud of witnesses. If you back up, you find chapter 11, which is the *Hebrews Hall of Faith*, describing the mighty saints of old. See, the Bible was not originally penned with chapters and verses. Those were added later for structure's sake. So really, original readers would have read about the saints of old in Hebrews 11 and then immediately jumped into the passage that says, "Therefore, since we are surrounded by so great a cloud of witnesses..." (saints of old) in chapter 12 and verse 1. We often do a mental break when we hop chapters and verses. We have a tendency to stop and start over while reading, when Scripture really wasn't written that way.

See, the cloud of witnesses is very unique. It's like when

Jesus ran into Elijah and Moses on the Mount of Transfiguration. Saints of old from the cloud of witnesses appeared! Everything in the Word is for us, and we want to keep chiseling away at the veil, if you will, which Jesus died to give us access to.

VARYING MANIFESTATIONS

You can have encounters *of* or *from* the divine. The manifestations of these encounters can vary widely. Here's a quick example. When Jesus was baptized in the Spirit, the heavens opened, the Holy Spirit came down in bodily form, and then He heard the voice of the Father, like we mentioned earlier. So this encounter was of the Holy Spirit, and the Holy Spirit manifested Himself in bodily form like a dove and came upon Jesus.

However, in Acts 2, this experience looked different for the disciples. Had they been fixated on the distinct model of Christ's Holy Spirit manifestation, I feel they could have missed the unique manner in which the Holy Spirit came in the upper room. He came like a rushing, mighty wind, and tongues as of fire sat upon each of them. This was totally distinct and uniquely different than past manifestation.

Don't get hung up on duplicating past methods and models. Be open to new and different ones. This groundwork, I believe, will broaden us in the same way that you broaden a runway so that an airplane can land. As we broaden ourselves, we'll be open to God landing upon us in new ways.

In Genesis 18, the Lord appeared with two angels near the great trees of Mamre to Abraham. You'll see in Scripture that angels often appear by trees. In Judges 6 it happens again with Gideon. Be mindful of these key features of manifestations. Furthermore, the Bible says they appeared near the great trees of Mamre while Abraham was at his tent entrance.

If you read real closely, it says three men appeared. Well, one was the Lord, and two were angels. You can see as you keep reading the chapters that follow, Abraham says, "Lord," and he stayed with the Lord Himself here. It's one of the few encounters where God Himself comes down into the earth. There are other instances, like when Jacob wrestles with God, for example. But Abraham never left the Lord's side. God manifested Himself personally, as well as brought angelic visitation in the midst of the encounter.

In Acts 23:11, Paul is in the prison cell and Jesus Christ Himself came and stood next to him in the cell and says to him, "Fear not, you'll go to Rome." In other words, *don't worry, your life here will be hemmed up. You still have to go to Rome.* And Jesus Christ Himself came that night and stood near Paul.

In Acts 9, Paul had the blinding light and encountered the Lord and he said, "Saul, Saul, why do you persecute Me?" This was Jesus. It wasn't the Father or the Holy Spirit, it was Jesus Christ. We read there was a blinding light and a voice, and many of us know the story. Paul had something like scales on his eyes for three days and didn't eat or drink anything.

So whether it's technically the Father God or the Holy Spirit or Jesus Himself or a mysterious account of the angelic or a saint of old—it's still a divine encounter. Don't write off the possibility of encountering God beyond a still, small voice. As you begin to expect divine encounters, open yourself to moments that are *of or from* the Lord that might look different than what you originally expected.

10

REVEALINGS AND RELOCATIONS

THE REVELATORY ENCOUNTERS

Throughout this book, we've talked plenty on commissioning encounters and how experiences with God tie into our callings. We've discussed the nature of encounters, several reasons for their happening, the covenant-core of encounters, and the apologetics to support their necessity.

One notable force behind encounters is *revelation*. Many times, an encounter won't pertain to your calling, destiny, or something about you. But a lot of times you'll have encounters for the sole purpose of *revelation*, which is paramount.

One of the encounters of many in Scripture where it was solely revelatory was with Daniel. You'll often see revelatory encounters around prophets. Not always, but it sure is prevalent in their lives, obviously, because they're mouthpieces for God. They're messengers, so they get revelation downloads, and they voice the very thing they just encountered and experienced. We see it with Ezekiel, Isaiah, Jeremiah, and Daniel.

I'll tell you this to encourage you, and I love this about people I run with; we're very different, and we know it and we appreciate that, in call, impartation, giftings, and what we carry. For instance, what I walk in predominantly and carry is vastly different than from, say, Todd White. And we know that. We'll get around each other and glean from one another and pull things out of the other. Same with Daniel Kolenda, or Michael Koulianos. And that's what the Body of Christ is like, that's the fullness.

I would encourage you, if you don't walk predominantly in the prophetic call, and the messenger/revelatory stuff is not as common for you, that's okay. Don't shun it. Too often believers stay too focused on where their strengths are because it's what's common to them, it's where they're comfortable, it's what's well known. So they'll just stay in their lane—rightfully so. However, on the one hand, you still need to broaden and better set yourself for the fullness of what all God has for you. Stretch out a bit and learn to dive into new depths.

Again, this is as the Lord leads. Don't try to make stuff happen, but as God enables you, allow yourself to experience revelatory encounters. Allow yourself to rub shoulders with people who have varying giftings that might look different than yours. Otherwise, we surround ourselves with like-minded people with like-minded vision, and that's amazing, but the fullness is lacking, and you get tunnel vision, and then we come to not quite appreciate what else is out there. Don't slip into an echo chamber like this.

So if you're lacking in the prophetic, I'd encourage you to get around prophets and the prophetic. You don't know anybody personally? Then go through YouTube videos and pull from the anointing. Maybe you're pastoral but you love the prophetic, well then ... dig into the prophetic. If you're prophetic and you want more teaching, then be just like a baby bird and pull from all of it where you can find it. As God enables true relationships, too, then take advantage of that. It's not a weird thing; it's a fullness of Jesus thing. They also need what you have, and you'll rub off on them.

I see a lot of these revelatory encounters happen with prophets, and you can get around them and rub shoulders and the same thing they walk in will get off onto you. The anointing is tangible. It's like a cold virus; it's alive and tangible and it will jump onto others and get on people. It's a literal frequency. It's like how Paul (Acts 19) had handkerchiefs touch his skin and when they came in contact with others, demons would shriek and leave people, and healings and miracles would take place. It's a tangible thing. I encourage you to go for it and get around what you can and for greater fullness.

Revelation by definition is *supernatural understanding, wisdom, knowledge from God.* In Daniel 10, we see one of the divine encounters in Scripture that most profoundly shows this. The text says he was in mourning for three weeks. He was on a twenty-one-day fast. That's where we get the Daniel fast from. He ate no bread or meat, and didn't even shave, nor did he anoint himself, which means he didn't bathe. He just straight up went into mourning.

A lot of people don't know this, and often get discouraged; I did at first. But if you read carefully, you'll notice it says he was in mourning for three weeks, not fasting. He ate vegetables and water, no bread, no meat, and especially had no delicacies of the kingdom, and he didn't bathe or shave. In the New Testament Jesus tells us to shave, comb our hair, and not to appear to anybody as though we're fasting (Matthew 6:17). So don't get hung up on this and think you need to grow your beard and not shower in your Daniel fast. It isn't legalism. But the idea in the New Testament fast is that you don't want people to know you're fasting, otherwise you'll lose your reward. So you appear to be clean-shaven and so forth. But we can talk about it amongst ourselves to strengthen and encourage one another in the Body of Christ, of course.

Anyway, sometimes during a Daniel fast that supernatural mourning will come upon you, and it's not because you just changed your diet, or a result of being sad now that you can't eat sweets. I'm talking a literal, tangible spirit of mourning. It's a supernatural thing. Don't fight it, but draw close to Jesus in those times. There's really no better way to get through it other than by clinging to Jesus, which is always the most fruitful decision you'll ever make in your life, anyway. I've experienced it way too many times on the Daniel fast. It's a tangible mourning. Why the Lord does it? I'm not sure. But I can tell you this, it sure births breakthrough and *revelation* like you wouldn't believe.

I believe it's a deep groaning of the Spirit that hits, and sometimes you don't know or understand or have any logic for it because it's a real tangible, spiritual thing that happens. I can tell you this, too; it's only going to lift when the time is ready to lift. So you just don't fight it, but instead cling to Jesus and pray and break through. It almost helps push you and drive you into Him.

I am uncertain who I heard say it, but fasting without prayer is mere starvation. You never see in Scripture where they just fast to do it to be a sacrificial thing. You're just starving yourself at that point, and it's just sheer sacrifice with no potency or reason to it. It's fasting coupled together with prayer which is one of the most dynamic tools we've been given.

A lot of people don't know this, and when they experience it for the first time during a Daniel fast, they get discouraged because they don't know what's going. But let me encourage you to not worry about it if that happens to you. I remember the first time it happened to me, I thought, *what is going on?* It went on for one day, then two, and before I knew it a week had passed. It stays with you and you start thinking you're stuck with it, and it can get a little scary, but God knows what He's doing.

So as Daniel finishes this three week fast, it was on the 24th day of the first month as he was standing on the bank of the Nile and Gabriel appeared to him. This is divine encounter of or from an angelic messenger, Gabriel, who said "I've come to make known to you the revelation/meaning of the vision"(Daniel 10:14, ESV).

So this divine encounter to Daniel was strictly for the sole purpose of bringing revelation that was paramount for his day. Daniel unlocked this seventy-year prophecy from Jeremiah by revelation. Had he not done that, that prophetic word would never have come to pass. So, revelation is so important in all seasons of life to stay in tune with the voice of God and destiny.

If you read closely in Ezekiel 8:3, you'll notice it says the hand of the Spirit of the Lord came down and grabbed Ezekiel by the locks of his hair and pulled him up between the heavens and the earth. This encounter wasn't for commissioning, because Ezekiel was already a full-out prophet of God. Daniel, in the example a moment ago, was already a seasoned prophet. So they're not all for *commissioning*; some are for *revelatory purposes*. As you dissect past encounters, you may see that at times, you had an encounter *after* a commissioning. You were already set on the course of your destiny, yet an encounter happened and came with revelation. These revelatory encounters are just as pivotal as a commissioning or empowerment encounter. Why didn't the Lord just tell Ezekiel directly? Because it's just how God does it. Sometimes He just wants an encounter and an experience.

Getting back to the text in Ezekiel, it says a hand of the Spirit of the Lord grabbed him by the locks of his hair between the heavens and the earth so he could see visions of God concerning Israel. He was having revelation about them.

I have had this experience before, where the hand of the

Spirit of the Lord came. I was in my bedroom in prayer. I know it sounds out there, but it grabbed me by my neck. Before I knew it, I started seeing my room through an out-of-body experience. So, my spirit was being taken out of my body, out of my room. How did I feel my neck get grabbed? I would believe the same way Ezekiel felt the locks of his hair get grabbed. If you read the text closely, you'll see he didn't go in body, but also had an out-of-body experience. When Paul talked of similar experiences in 2 Corinthians, he said, "whether in the body or out, I don't know," so the exact dynamics of how it happened don't seem to be as important as the fact it happened. I only believe and know Ezekiel had an experience in his spirit, not his body, because it's how it happened with me. It can be challenging to explain spiritual things with carnal intellect.

The hand of the Spirit of the Lord grabs the spirit man, but in the spirit, you still have a physical makeup. How else do you believe that we "see" a cloud of witnesses? Moses and Elijah appeared to Jesus. How do you think we are created in God's image? When we go to heaven, we're not just going to see blurry spirit people floating around. We're going to see physical people with hair, skin, and glorified bodies, of course. Even Jesus Christ is glorified in the book of Revelation; He still has hair, a face, eyes, feet, and so on. So there's still these attributes in the Spirit, and the Spirit grabs us by them. The spirit world is so real, that literally the Spirit needs something to grab on to.

In my encounter, I had virtually the same experience. The Lord actually did it to me on the Hebrew calendar on the eighth month and the third day, tied into the account in Ezekiel 8:3. He just synced it up so perfectly for me. When I came out of it, I was so dumbfounded and taken aback. I just had no grid for it. I've always had short hair and have never grown it long. If you're a guy and have long hair and it looks good on you, great. I've never had anything against it. I just always felt it more of a hassle, personally, more than anything. But I digress. I had no locks to grab on to, so I was grabbed by the throat. I realize this may be difficult and a little out there for some readers. I heard someone once explain it to me like this, and I loved the analogy. They said, "It's like pulling a Kleenex out of a box. You can feel the box still, which would be the body, and the vibration of it, but the Kleenex is also very real on the inside of that box, like the spirit. But the physical source of the Kleenex box getting pulled out, you can feel both. You feel the vibrations and the resistance from the box, and the Kleenex being pulled out, as well."

It's not a perfect analogy, but it's very similar, ironically enough. You can tangibly feel your spirit leaving your body. And it's scriptural, as well. Paul says it clearly when recounting his experience in 2 Corinthians. Out-of-body experiences were meant for God's creation, initially, by the supernatural, but the demonic just took it and ran with it, and still does. But I believe this is what is going on in Ezekiel 8:3.

In that encounter of mine, I'm in my bed because I was in prayer anyway, waiting in silence, and it happened suddenly. And then I could feel it. There's this pull and you can feel almost the 'brush' of the natural and the spiritual separating. It's a tangible, and very real thing. As this happens, I'm seeing my room, my bedroom door right in front of me the same way I'm positioned, but my spiritual eyes are opening now. My physical body was still back in silence, eyes closed. I could see my bedroom door as I leave the room, and it's very surreal. I was suspended in the air and could see the stars, just like in Ezekiel 8:3, in between the heavens and the earth. Ezekiel didn't say this just because it was convenient to say, but his spirit went between the heavens and the earth, and he knew it because you can see the separation between the two.

To be absent from the body is to be present with the Lord, according to 2 Corinthians 5:6. The spirit is the life of all that you are. When your spirit leaves, there's nothing else. This body is just a physical container for the spirit, so when it leaves, and I'm not referring to for eternity's sake or death, but for a spiritual experience, the body is like a rag doll. There's nothing there. I heard John Paul Jackson share about how when he came out of his body and his wife at first would freak out. She'd shake him, and he was "not there." He was off in heaven having some experience, but he, himself, was not there. The first few times this happened, she thought he was dead, and freaking out, but he would come back and ask her, "What?!" and she'd yell at him to never do that again.

Another reason I think God often does this is that He separates your spirit from your physical soul, which is more carnal. It's your mind, will, and emotions that can be earthly.

It's easier when your spirit gets separated; there's no consciousness to fight it. Your mind, will, and emotions and natural man fight the spirit, like what happens in visions sometimes. It starts to blur things, but you can see so much more clearly that it's pure spirit when it gets taken out of the body. It's pure spirit communication, and it's so clear.

So on this occasion, the same thing happened. It was a divine encounter for revelation; as I was taken into this vision. I was foreshown a thing that was about to happen that was a big deal, and nobody knew, and I won't get into it in print, but sure enough it happened how I had foreseen. But I mention it in detail here because it happened for revelation. God so desired to give revelation on this topic that He took my spirit out of my body to show me what He wanted to show me.

After the journey, your spirit going back into your body, on the other hand, is kind of like a collision, and there is a very real reunification that takes place. Not that they're all the same, but I remember that first time, it was so real. Due to the way I'm wired, I can't do crazy movement, like roller coasters, because I get dizzy so easily. I could go running in a few circles and be dizzy for half a day. I love heights, and stuff like that, which don't bother me at all. Things that go straight up or straight down, I can handle, but fast and sudden turning, not so much. So getting sucked up and suspended between the heavens and the earth real fast was so real to me, like a full-blown roller-coaster ride. When I came back, I kid you not, but my equilibrium was shot. I could tangibly feel it as I emerged back into my body, so much so that I took a couple of Tylenol. Sometimes I think we believe the spirit is just an "out there" thing, but it's actually more real than the temporal and natural.

The apostle John obviously had a *revelatory* encounter when he got caught up while on the island of Patmos. The whole book of Revelation was written from that encounter. It was a revelation encounter that declared things to come, many of which have already come to pass. So God literally closed out the whole book for us to know the future of what's coming by *an encounter*. John was already an apostle, so this wasn't a commissioning encounter, and it wasn't an empowerment, either, but a *revelatory* encounter.

You can read an encounter in the Bible, but experiencing it is a whole other matter. If you've never ridden a roller coaster in your life, but just read about them, and never actually experienced anything that went up and down or fast and around sharp turns, do you think you would have *true* understanding? No. Not until you get in the car and are flying upside down. Experience is one of the best teachers, even though we do the best we can with revelation from the Spirit while reading the Word. That's why I stress so much that as you read the Scripture and come across encounters and experiences that intrigue you and stir hunger, camp out on them.

Ask God for encounters like them and tell Him, "I've got to have one like that. Please let me experience that." Learn to experience the Word and let the Word experience you. You'll find that revelation will freely flow in the midst of these ecstatic happenings.

11

EMPOWERMENT AND EXPANSION
FILLED AND BEING FILLED

We desperately need the Spirit, strength, power, and grace to flow into what the Lord has called us to. This is where empowerment encounters come into play. You might say, "Yeah, but we have the Holy Spirit. The same Spirit that raised Christ from the dead is within us. Isn't that all we need?" Remember, with God, it's never *either/or*, but He is a *both/and* kind of God.

Not only that, but empowerment encounters are biblical. The Lord doesn't just give us general empowerment through His indwelling presence, but specific empowerment for His unique purposes. May this chapter enlighten you a little more to the biblical nature of the installments of God's empowering presence for every task.

We know Acts 2 as the chapter that describes the Holy Spirit being poured out on the day of Pentecost, which is a great example of an empowerment encounter. If you remember, Jesus had already sent out the twelve disciples (see Matthew 10), and the seventy-two (see Luke 10), and had already given them a commission. Yet He then said once He left that they would need another power from above. The power of the Holy Spirit's baptism.

You might be reading this and have never been filled with the Holy Spirit, and that's okay. I want to believe with you for that, or perhaps a fresh infilling. You may be thinking, *Well, Brian, I have been filled with the Spirit before, and I don't need to be again because I've already got the Spirit.* That may be, but that's not biblical. Biblical principles point to being filled with the Spirit perpetually (see Ephesians 5). If we really break it down, we're to be continually filled with the Spirit, and that's why Jesus said, "If you abide in Me (which is a continual thing), you will experience a continual abiding in intimacy." It's not a one-time stop-and-shop deal, but a relationship.

Let's look at the text:

"When the day of Pentecost arrived, they were all together in one place. And suddenly there came from heaven a sound like a mighty rushing wind, and it filled the entire house where they were sitting. And divided tongues as of fire appeared to them and rested on each one of them. And they were all filled with the Holy Spirit and began to speak in other tongues as the Spirit gave them utterance" (Acts 2:1-4, ESV).

So we see they were *all* filled with the Spirit. The manifestations were the sound of a mighty rushing wind, and tongues of fire appearing. This is exactly what Jesus had told them; to wait until they had been endued with power from on high. To me, a true sign of the Holy Spirit is power, not only the grace and the ability to walk in power, but manifest power, not just tongues, although we want it all. But the true biblical precedent that Jesus set was *power* coming from a Holy Spirit encounter.

That one word, *power*, is an obvious *empowerment encounter*. I want to encourage you, dear reader, to never walk around in doubt, thinking that you don't have what it takes. Obviously, you should always be pressing in for more. Yet, I don't want you to think we are insinuating that you don't have another and you're an encounter or two short of being powerful enough to do the will of God.

If you're a believer, you have the Kingdom of God within you, the Bible says, and you have the same Spirit that raised Jesus from the dead (see Romans 8), so go for it! That's one of the things about our ministry. I always tell people, the youngest ones to the oldest ones, "You've got the Holy Spirit; you can do it. Prophesy and heal the sick, cast out devils. Go for it!"

However, those things don't negate the reality that there's also a real biblical dynamic of a *continual* infilling of the Spirit and greater levels of power by the same Spirit. We are both filled with the Spirit and *being* filled with the Spirit. We *both* have power *and* are experiencing new power in new encounters.

So this type of encounter, in a nutshell, is literally God coming upon people in a manifest way by divine encounter to empower them. You come out of it in greater boldness, a greater flowing of gifts. It's an impartation. It happens in meetings, conferences, it happens in the secret place, wherever and whenever God chooses. But this is also what I want to encourage you to contend for while we still go in the Gospel and the fullness of what we already have.

A lot of times people teach that there is no more to obtain and that we have it all. I get it, and it's true to a degree. But there are layers of truth, and there are installments of Kingdom realities, and empowerment encounters are a biblical principle. We've been glorified in Christ, yet we are going from glory to glory to greater glory. We've been given strength in Jesus, yet we are moving from strength to strength. Don't find yourself in one ditch or the other.

My fear in the belief that you have everything you need already, is that you might just stop there. I don't ever want to see growth stunted and power to become stagnant in the name of "I have everything I need already." Instead, take that principle and couple it together with the reality that there is more to contend for. Couple it with the reality that the disciples were filled with the Holy Spirit once, yet continually filled with the Spirit. Otherwise, you'll shortchange yourself. Don't go dormant by riding on last season's revelation or the past year's empowerment. Contend for a fresh wind!

After the empowerment in Acts 1, fast-forward to Acts 4:27, and we see another empowerment encounter. Let's look at verse 13, which is gold for the secret place:

"Now when they saw the boldness of Peter and John, and perceived that they were uneducated, common men, they were astonished. And they recognized that they had been with Jesus" (Acts 4:13, ESV).

There it is. Common, uneducated Peter and John had a boldness on them that astonished folks, and the light bulb switched on; these guys had been with Jesus! That's always the go-to: intimacy and being with Jesus.

For backdrop and context before we get into verse 27, I want to point out that persecution always leads to greater authority. It's just the enemy's nature, but he always does it anyway. You killed Jesus, and now you open up the resurrection power of salvation for all of mankind. To persecute the Body of Christ is utter foolishness, but the enemy does it every time. The enemy is the king of checkmating himself. He goes on the opposition, battling, and he always gets himself in the checkmate move of God. Persecute the Church, and God will give us grace and greater boldness.

These are the best days to live in, right now. To persecute the Church is like a bad weed; you go to pull it out, but the seeds from pulling it out spread more and there's ten more weeds. You just can't stop the authentic Church. When you see it affected, then it probably wasn't authentic from the start. But if it's from the Spirit, you can't quench it. You won't be able to stop it. You go to persecute it by killing one, ten more are born. It just doesn't work. You martyr ten, a hundred more are born. It just doesn't work, and that's what you see here in the fourth chapter of Acts. The enemy always overplays his hand.

I want to encourage you in the hard times, specifically created by the enemy against you through persecution, if you hold true to the upright ways of God in your posture with Him, in holiness, purity, and loving Jesus, you'll experience what life was meant to be. Stay the course, and the pressure of life will turn a coal into a diamond every time.

So, in verse 27, Peter and John had just gotten locked up in jail for speaking with boldness. Persecution had hit the Church hard, but verse 27 says the believers are crying out to God about the persecution. Mind you, in Acts 2 the Holy Spirit came, and Jesus said previously they would receive power. Fast-forward to two chapters later, and they're facing greater persecution now. This is part of the dynamics of greater installments of God infilling them. I think a lot of it is us getting more out of the way, if you will, as part of getting in full alignment with God. All the things within us that hinder the full flow of God, soulish things, motives, and so forth, are removed and greater grace comes. The Scripture says:

"When they were released, they went to their friends and reported what the chief priests and the elders had said to them. And when they heard it, they lifted their voices together to God" (Acts 4:23-24, ESV).

Then jumping to verse 29 and 30, we see they're still praying:

"And now, Lord, look upon their threats and grant to your servants to continue to speak your word with all boldness, while you stretch out your hand to heal, and signs and wonders are performed through the name of your holy servant Jesus" (Acts 4:29-30, ESV).

Again, you do not persecute God's Church. That's the biggest no-no. We are always the dominant force in the globe. I don't care who it is, how high the rank, how big they talk. And that's not an arrogance thing; it's confidence when it's in God. He's everything. He is the most powerful source of the Holy Ghost in and through men 100,000 percent of the time, every day all day.

Now they're crying out to the Lord to look upon the threats being made against their servants. Verse 31 says, "And when they had prayed, the place in which they were gathered together was shaken." A full-out, supernatural, mini earthquake hit from their prayers unto God. But look at what it says next, "And they were all filled with the Holy Spirit and continued to speak the word of God with boldness" (Acts 4:31, ESV). Here's another filling of the Holy Spirit when they had already had it in chapter 2 just previously.

All of heaven resides in you. John G. Lake used to wake up and look in the mirror and say, "God lives in that man, and he is in God." He would talk to himself in the mirror that God lives in that man. They say his revelation of God in man was remarkable and he moved in crazy power. Yet a continual infilling was also a reality in his life.

Never feel like you've arrived. Also refuse to feel like you come up short. Live in the divine tension of knowing that you're filled while also chasing a continual infilling. Operate day to day in the love of God and the Gospel and the

Kingdom like all heaven is in you, because it is. Again, you have the same Spirit living in you that raised Christ from the dead. But don't ever let that stop you from contending and crying out for increase.

Also, be aware that hard times often push you into elevated situations of crying out to God in which He hits the land even harder. I love that the Scripture says when they prayed together the place was shaken. Despite being filled in Acts 2, they're filled again in Acts 4. Now it speaks of the apostles, operating in what's called *great power*. Don't ever think that's by accident. Every word of Scripture is chosen by God. In Acts 2, power comes. In Acts 4, the apostles were operating in *great* power. Great grace was upon them. Do you see the expansion of empowerment taking place?

I'VE SEEN ADDITIONAL WAVES OF EMPOWERMENT IN MY OWN life. At times I may have walked in power and then subsequent encounters cause me to operate in *great power* as the Scriptures describe. Now, don't get ahead of yourself. Be grateful and content in all things. Paul said to be content in all seasons (see Philippians 4). Don't compare yourself or your experience to someone else's and become imbalanced in your approach.

It's important not to get ahead of yourself. Generally speaking, the people flowing in great power have seen a few more battles and persecution than others. Not always, but often. So be warned that upon praying for great grace, great trial can come as well. Like we established earlier, sometimes commissioning encounters are given to cling onto because of the trying times that are to come. Likewise, empowerment encounters can contain the same purpose.

You've likely been around people who operate in great grace, favor, and blessing, and it seems like everything they do works. The choices they make, the doors they go through, it seems easy and like nothing backfires or goes haywire. And you wonder, *how does that work?* That's when people are operating in great grace. There's just favor on them, doors are opened, and there's ease along with the acceleration of favor. It has nothing to do with their craftiness or performance. It's unmerited favor. We see these folks and it's like they're never going into lack, they're always increasing. That's always God's ultimate will for us, but we're all in different seasons, and that's okay too. We are all growing and going for more.

I have had many seasons where there not only wasn't great grace, but there was zero power. I remember one time going up to a crew of deaf people in a Walmart parking lot and just having them all look at me funny as nothing happened and I walked off. I couldn't even pray for them, much less see them healed. But when these things happen, you stay faithful and steady and obey Jesus. He's walking on water, so you walk on water; if He takes a left step, you take one.

The battles come, persecution will come, but you stay faithful and keep walking. Don't worry about what anybody thinks. You just know you heard the Word of the Lord and you obey. Before you know it, that power becomes *greater* power. Persecution and resistance from the enemy will come, but it makes you stronger. Then that power goes into great power, and that authority goes from influence in a city, to influence in a state or province, and then from that to a nation, and eventually *nations*.

Faith is like a mustard seed and has the ability to grow. The measure of faith we have been given is to be grown, watered, and expanded. It's all throughout Scripture. This isn't a one-and-done thing. It's the process of maturity, a walking out your salvation. Again, not to mitigate, minimize, or negate the mentality of Jesus having paid it all and everything being accessible, because it totally is. We have all riches in Christ. Yet the Kingdom is a progressive thing, as is our faith, and the measures and authority that we grow in.

So you'll begin to notice as you stick with it that this power and authority will become greater power and authority through continual encounter. And this grace goes into great grace. Strength becomes great strength. In the midst of pursuit, do the best you can to be content because you may be walking in grace, yet you get around people who are walking in *great* grace, and you may start to think, *Man, am I doing something wrong?* As a result, jealousy and envy can kick in, and you never want to go there in any way. You want to admire, honor, love, support, and bless, while perpetually chasing after more.

In fact, the protocol of heaven is for us to honor what God is doing in others. As a result, we'll find ourselves being drawn into those same redemptive realities. You don't ever want to backbite, cut, or get jealous and let nasty things creep into your heart. Let it encourage you, and say, "Yep, that's where I'm going!" Bless and honor them, and you'll see yourself being pulled right in to it. If you want what someone has, don't *envy* it—*honor* it.

12
ENCOUNTERS AND EXPERIENCES
PERSONAL MOMENTS OF ENCOUNTER

Heaven is attracted to itself. I love that about God. As you just begin to lean in from the interior, He manifests in mighty ways. With some of my covenant brothers I run with, we'll spark up certain conversations on purpose with each other just to trigger God. Someone might object and say God's not like a concession machine, but that's not how we look at it. We love Him and want Him, and we know how God is attracted to mankind above all creation. He's so infatuated with us, but it's an interior posture and attention turning to Him and He shows up.

We'll just share encounters and experiences or fresh revelation on purpose, and it's just profound how God can show up to encourage you, even through conversation. I'm reminded of a dear friend of mine I went to Bible college with, who many don't know because he's not popular on the scene and heaven has him hidden, named Brian Jackson. He went to the mission field in Africa, and now lives in Wisconsin. He's raised the dead, seen miracles, you name it, this guy is just ridiculous! In a good way, of course. We've kept in touch over the years while living far apart, but there would be times when we'd get together and just lean into God and heaven would sneak in and smash us. I mean, we never knew how He was going to come and in what manner, but time and time again, heaven would just sneak in and take over in these profound ways of encounter. I just love that. I dare you to try it yourself with your friends. Make time to talk about heaven. Year after year, whether it's my house or Brian's, I'd be with him and we'd be up late and all of a sudden heaven would sneak in.

Make it your mission to share your experiences and encounters. Don't bottle them. Granted, some encounters are for your eyes only. The Lord might direct you to keep silent on an encounter, either for a season or permanently. That's not what we are talking about. When an experience happens, share it. Not only will it create hunger in others, but it can also release impartations and attract heaven all over again.

Now that we've established eleven chapters of biblical foundation and exposition, I wish to share in this closing chapter some personal experiences with you. I love what these release and impart when I share them in meetings and trainings. So, it's my prayer that you'll have similar encounters and experiences, or at the very least, hunger for them as you read. I pray that as you read this, God would loose things, right now, wherever you are reading these words, and that moving forward, stuff would just snap and break open in your life in *greater ways*.

THE FALCON

The first experience I had was late in November 2004. Up to this point, there weren't any really notable encounters in my life that I can recall. Definitely God speaking, fasting, prayer, I'd been in Bible college, but I could only remember one single prophetic dream that I could recount while in Bible college.

Some people are just born with it, inherently, but I was not that guy. I'd seen gold dust already, but otherwise, no visions. Nothing. But as far as a destiny-impact type view, it actually got to the point where I was realizing that, and I started to see these encounters in God in the Bible and how they were flipping people upside down. Moses + burning bush = deliverer of all Israel. Joshua + angel of the Lord of hosts = conquering the Promised Land. Gideon + angel under his father's tree = taking out the Midianites. Paul + a blinding light = apostle to the Gentiles. On and on it went; I couldn't escape it. I started seeing these in the written Word, and I noticed this common thread.

This is also why I love encounters so much, because it's just God's way, and He loves to touch His people. Not that you have to, but I just think it's amazing, and why not? He's no respecter of persons. So, I had sought God and really felt this experience coming, I could just sense it. I want to interject here for a moment and say sometimes you can seek yourself into one. Don't feel like everything is sovereignly set up by heaven and until you hit that certain day, it's not going to happen. He's a rewarder of those who *diligently* seek Him. You could just about seek your way into one, I'm telling you. That's not to say He's a concession machine and we can just put a quarter in and then get what we want, but also, He doesn't bypass extreme spiritual hunger very often, I'll say that.

I had seen it long enough throughout Scripture, and modern-day men and women who I respect who've impacted the globe. So, the *Reader's Digest* version of the story: I was seeking heaven really hard up until this point, and I felt Him call me to go to this conference in Dallas, Texas. I can't remember what the name of it was, but there were powerful men and women of God there. Day one, two, three, you could feel the veil was thin. I knew I was close to having some type of run-in with God, and it was going to shift everything. To be honest with you, all I knew in Bible college, I was thinking some type of Smith Wigglesworth mantle was going to come and it was going to be all this dead-raising power or some time type of John G. Lake anointing. That's all I knew at the time. And that's one thing you can never predetermine, what your call is, nor can you pick and choose, and thank God for that because like we've established earlier, you just won't have a grace for anything else anyway. You don't need to fight it; just welcome Him, and be open.

So the first three days go by, and there's laying on of hands every session, and it seemed as though nothing noteworthy was happening. Other people were getting rocked, but not me. The very last session, I was thinking, *this has got to be it.* The people leading the conference were coming around to where I was standing, laying hands on people, and bodies were flying every which way. They came to me, and they laid hands on me, and nothing happened. So, to be honest with you, I left that night a bit frustrated. I was thinking to myself, *Man, this was supposed to be it. Why did I even come here?* Despite this, I do think some kind of impartation happened to me at the conference though.

After this I left Dallas, Texas and headed to Houston, where I was living at the time. So, at this time I was on the interstate going about 80 mph in a full-size white Expedition SUV, in flatland Texas, with not a single hill in sight, and no other cars around. You couldn't miss me. I will never forget what happened next. Remember, I had left the conference very frustrated, but I thought, *oh well, I'm not backing down. There's no plan B for me here. I don't know if you recognize yet, God, but I don't have another option here. You will not stop hearing from me until I have some type of run-in.* God loves that type of hunger and it doesn't make Him nervous at all. So I was doing that kind of pouting for about thirty minutes, then turned on that worship CD and started praying in tongues and planned on doing that for the whole three-hour drive.

I was about halfway there, and I'll never forget what happened next. I reached down really quick with my right hand to get something to drink, while I was praying in tongues to the old Brian and Jenn Johnson CD, *Undone*, I think. I came up with my drink, and suddenly this huge falcon of some sort, probably two feet in height with a wingspan of six feet, showed up and took up the whole windshield. It flew down out of the east while I was driving. It literally swooped down, while I was going 80 mph, and spread its wings and covered the whole windshield, just like that.

It happened so fast—it literally turned its head as it was flying, swooped down, and looked through the glass with both eyes looking straight at my eyes. It was almost like a haunting, but in a good way. I could tell it was there with great purpose. This was not some accidental huge bird flying to catch a mouse in a field and just happened to see this huge white SUV on the way. That was not what was going on! This thing swept down on purpose and its eyes pierced mine as it looked at me through the windshield. Just as soon as it looked me in the eyes, I freaked out and logic kicked in, and I thought he was going to come busting in my windshield due to the speed I was traveling at. I could see things getting ugly with broken glass flying everywhere.

I swerved fast all the way across the wake-up bumps on the road. Thank goodness there were no other cars around, or things could have been even worse! As a result, I just missed him. I swerved back into my lane, certain that I had clipped him. I thought I caught its wing or something. I thought I had seen him rolling on the highway. I looked back through all my car's mirrors, rearview and side-view, and I didn't see him anywhere. No bird carcass rolling around on the road. Nothing, nowhere. I looked up in the air, and saw nothing there, either. I don't know what happened to this day.

It had too much spiritual juice on it, if you know what I mean. It just felt like God was in that, and I didn't know what was going on. It was a good feeling, and I knew it was set up by God. It wasn't just an "oh, that was neat" moment or something in the natural that just happened. So, I kid you not, for the next half hour, I continued driving down the interstate, with my jaw on the floor, just dumbfounded. The experience just had that substance to it, as though God was behind it. I finally got the thought to ask God, which I hadn't even prayed out loud yet, "What was that about?" As the thought was starting to go through my mind, I realized I was passing by an eighteen-wheeler truck that had these full eagle/falcons on each of its mud flaps behind the tires, each with spread wings just looking at me. I hadn't even finished my thought of asking God about the bird from half an hour ago when I saw more of them on mud flaps next to me.

When I got home, I didn't even tell anybody close to me about this experience for a while because I was still digesting it. Lo and behold, not long after, I went into a dream during a period of fasting. I don't know the exact time, but I think it was around 1:30 a.m. at the end of November. So I went into this dream, and this guy told me the future. I started seeing visions and prayer. The seer realm opened up as a result, and now dreams, visions, and prophetic pictures are something our ministry carries strongly.

We get around people and it breaks open in their lives as

well. The Lord sent a falcon to fly in front of my car and run me off the road, and more importantly, pierce me in my eyes while I'm driving, which represents a destiny and a call. After this and the dream, I looked up the falcon, all of them—golden eagle, bald eagle, red-tailed hawk—all the big falcon birds. A consistent theme in this family of birds that ties them all together is this attribute of keen eyesight. It was a prophetic picture of my spiritual eyes being opened in a new way.

So I want to encourage you, as you press in, or have had encounters, dissect what they mean as you encounter God now moving forward. I've already said it, but it bears repeating: you can't impart what you don't have. Encounters impart things. They make covenants and promises, but they also impart the very substance of the experience, which is why God does this. Now, as a result, you are a new person walking in this realm, and you have a depth of it that now just rubs off and overlaps into everything you do.

THE BLINDING LIGHT

In this next experience, I'm going to touch on the installment aspect of the encounters in my life. That experience with the falcon on the interstate really opened up the prophetic in my life and ministry. I don't do the title-dropping thing a whole lot, and you'll rarely ever hear me refer to myself as a prophet. I get referred to as one quite a bit, and that's okay. I see the need for it at times, but I just love Jesus and don't get caught up in title dropping. But I've been called everything, including evangelist, but in truth, the titles don't matter to me. But in actuality, that encounter in 2004 birthed the prophetic and even the office which we've walked in for years.

Fast-forward to late 2010, and in the years since that night on the interstate. I had been walking in the prophetic and honing in on the gift, increase in foreseeing elections and natural events, including catastrophes and things. But before that encounter in 2004, I could only remember *one* dream. Let that encourage you.

The five-fold gift of the prophet was the least of my favorite of the gifts. That was not what I wanted to be. That never leaves you, but that's what's amazing too; there are installments and things change.

By this time in 2010, I had had plenty of experiences that mattered in many ways, but as far as commissioning encounters, another major one was when I was preaching up in Northern California, north of Redding. I was in a conversation with a certain person in the middle of the day, not being spiritual at all. We weren't in prayer or doing anything profound.

Then, in mid-conversation, all of the sudden, the Lord decided to stiff-arm the conversation by coming into it and I went into a full vision. I saw Jesus in heaven looking down at me. It was as though He pulled out a circular cutout of heaven's floor. Then, after a moment, He pulled it back briefly, and as He did that He was looking at me, and this glorious, blinding light came out. When He pulled it back, it was like the barrier between heaven and earth was removed. I could still see Him, but I could also see the person I was in mid-conversation with.

It was so real in the vision, in the natural I quickly waved my arms like I was trying to keep something from hitting me in the face, and squinted, and the person I was talking with got shocked with power. They couldn't see the vision I went into, but power hit them. They thought I had somehow done something to them. You know how you do stuff that attracts static electricity? They didn't know what happened. All I did was wave my arms away from my face and I grabbed for my phone. This person didn't know yet what had happened or what I had seen.

So I come out of this vision and checked my phone to see that it was 12:01 p.m. One minute past noon. All I could think was, *what was that about?* I hadn't a clue, but I journaled it immediately and took down all the details I could without yet knowing what it fully meant.

After the trip, a month or two went by and I was still trying to sift through this particular encounter, but it was a bit sealed until the second part of it happened. In the beginning of 2011 I was scheduled to be preaching in Blacksburg, Virginia, and the Lord had called me to go into a forty-day fast that was going to end on the very day I got there to preach on a campus at Virginia Tech for a conference.

I had seen a vision of the underwater ways from Noah's flood, like how in Genesis it says waters burst up from the deep first, then the heavens opened. If you read the account of the flood really closely, waters from underground burst up first, then the heavens opened. I had seen a vision that was for where I was going to preach, but it also tied in to the exact fast I was going into. It was ironic enough that I was already on this forty-day fast and I saw this vision, and I looked up at my calendar and remembered I was going to be preaching in Virginia on February 17. The seventeenth day of the second month.

I knew God was tying in the Noah's flood vision to where I was going to be preaching with sin and repentance that needed to happen in this area. I started looking up the flood, and if you look closely at the text, it says it was the seventeenth day of the second month when the waters burst up and the flood began (see Genesis 7:11). Again, notice how highly specific God is when He moves, speaks, or does anything profound.

So I started checking the time, and mind you, I was already into this fast, and I was coming up to preach anyway when I learned this, and I was just trying to track the revelation so I knew what to release when I got there. It turns out this whole thing was a setup. I didn't even know what God was doing, to be honest with you. I was just tracking enough to know as a mouthpiece what to release when I got there.

So the time comes, and I got up there with a good friend of mine I was doing this forty-day fast together with, and when we arrived, I preached repentance that night. Lo and behold, I come to learn there's two waterways that run under the campus I'm preaching at. That's what I was seeing bursting up in a parable relating to Noah's flood and to the exact date in Scripture that I was going to be there. Now, it was eighty-plus degrees on campus in the middle of

February. I'll never forget this because people were playing volleyball in their shorts, riding their bikes on campus, shirts off, riding skateboards and other things as though it were summer on this college campus. That night in the meeting, feathers were manifesting, and it got strong, but I had to preach repentance and what God said into the area. We led it through prayer, and it concluded the forty-day fast.

We woke up the next day and there was a freak snowstorm that took everybody by surprise. It was the biggest temperature shift from one day to the next that had happened in over eighty years in that area. It was an atmospheric wonder that hit from preaching repentance; snow represents the purity of God and holiness. Ironically enough, its thickest point, like the epicenter, was right where we were at in Blacksburg. By the campus there was eight inches of snow, and as you went away from campus it got thinner. We were watching the news and even the local meteorologists were blown away and referring to it as a freak thing. This wonder in the atmosphere confirmed the word.

Since it had been almost a century since the last time something like this had happened, the current meteorologists didn't have a recent comparison to work from, so they thought there was no way the snow would stay on the ground because it was so hot the day before. They were predicting it would melt as the day went on, and that there was no way it would build. But it built so thick, it was a full-blown blanket. One day people were in shorts playing volleyball, and the next day people were sledding down the hills of the campus. It was a full-blown phenomenon. I thought that was the end of it. It was wild enough having heaven back the word I had for this region. Just that alone was way bigger than I anticipated.

Later that night as the sun was setting, my friend and I had ended our forty-day fasts, so we were smashing our faces with everything in front of us. Anything we could find. I'm either feast or fast, and especially after completing a fast, I'll eat anything in sight! So we found this Pizza Hut and decided to head inside. After we finished and we were heading outside, I decided I wanted to get a picture of this crazy wonder that we had seen all over the news that day. Right outside there was this table that was perfect—it was covered with eight inches of snow that nobody had touched and was high enough that it could be in the photo. I was not being spiritual at all; I merely thought how I wanted to capture this wonder in a picture. I've got the picture of this in my other book, *God of Wonders*, for reasons you'll understand in a moment.

So I gave my phone to an employee from Pizza Hut and asked him to take a picture of my friend and me but didn't specifically say I wanted the table in the picture. We just stood in front of it. So we were cheesing for the camera, and the employee took the picture. He got a puzzled look on his face as he looked at the phone and told us to hold on a moment. "I don't understand. What's going on?" he said. He handed the phone back to me, and as I went to look at it, this full-blown glory beam, whiter than the snow with almost a blue hue to it, was coming out of the heavens right over my shoulder. It baffled the mind of this Pizza Hut worker, who was scratching his head, wondering how this happened.

He took another photo, and everything was back to normal, and he said, "Oh, you know what I think happened is this light fixture on the wall over there on the brick wall showed up in the picture." If you look at the original image, you can see this one incandescent light bulb on the wall with a yellow hue to it that literally had nothing to do with the Q beam coming out of heaven. So we've got it caught on photo, as I was up there in Virginia when this snow wonder manifested as we released this word.

This is why you really need to track with heaven. Heaven is really like a Sherlock Holmes story in many ways. God is very strategic, calculated, and provides puzzle-piece type mysteries in what He does. So this photo was so crazy and undeniable. William Branham was one of the main people known for glory light showing up over his photos and they would have professional photographers inspect them. They would conclude that the light showed up supernaturally and that there was no other way light could have appeared on the film. This image was like one of those.

So just with the hustle and bustle of the trip, I got home, and started to seek God about this, because I was still trying to sift together this experience from California with the glory Q beam that came down from heaven and blinded me as I saw Jesus. I was still mulling over that one and still didn't understand it yet. When I got home, I realized this blue hue in the image was the glory Q beam I saw in California that day three months prior. It was a three-month timespan; I'll never forget it.

Remember how I checked the time and it was 12:01 p.m. when that happened? In that first part, I saw the Lord pull back the veil, I got blinded by a light, and someone else experienced the encounter and got shocked. Then three months later I was in Virginia, in a certain region that triggered that same blinding light that I already saw by visionary experience, but this time it was captured in a supernatural photo when I was trying to capture an atmospheric wonder that was released from the Word.

I went after heaven hard about this. Some people may think, *Wow, that's so awesome*, and move on without dissecting their encounters enough to find out what God is doing and why. For that reason I leaned into it and God started unpacking all of it to me.

I had to go back to the foundation of everything. So, blinding light; I've seen this before, and of course I've already mentioned this before, but the only place in all of Scripture with Jesus being involved with a blinding light from heaven is with the apostle Paul. Sometimes God will mimic a similar encounter from Scripture.

So I started going back into it and tracking the encounter with Paul and the blinding light since this is a comparable encounter to what Paul had. When I was on the West Coast, I got the vision, but then it was made manifest on the East Coast when I was in Virginia. It's like God waited on purpose, and then He hit that region. It got caught on camera, allowing me to have what I had already seen in a visionary experience.

We've all read the book of Acts, but this time I noticed this one detail I had never seen before. If you read Acts 26:12, Paul is before King Agrippa, telling him of his experience on the way to Damascus, elaborating on what happened in chapter 9 of Acts.

"In this connection, I journeyed to Damascus with the authority and commission of the chief priests. It was about noon that day, O King, I saw on the way a blinding light from heaven, brighter than the sun, that shone around me and those who journeyed with me. We had fallen to the ground, and I heard a voice saying" (Acts 26:12, ESV).

I had never seen that before. If you look in all of Scripture, Paul knew the exact time it happened; at about noon that day a blinding light came from heaven. We all know the encounter. That's where Paul received a commission encounter, and a sending to a people (the Gentiles). That's why I was not having a spiritual conversation and all of the sudden heaven was mimicking a similar experience.

That's why it's really key to track the details of encounters: *why, when, and how*. I was in the middle of a conversation with another person, and God was like, "Nope." There's noon! We cross noon that day, and *boom*, I go into a full vision, Jesus pulling back the heavens, a blinding light hits me, someone's with me just like there was someone with Paul, and they get taken into the experience, and in my case it was by a shock of power. By the time I came out of it, I check my phone to see it was 12:01. "At about noon that day, O King Agrippa." So God was waiting that day around noon to take me into an encounter. I took it further and realized that it was more of an apostolic commissioning. So like I mentioned, seven years prior there was more of the prophetic commissioning given from the falcon encounter. Like I mentioned in previous chapters, Paul was a teacher and prophet for a while in ministry before stepping into an apostolic role after the laying on of hands in Acts 14. I felt that this was a new installment for my life and destiny.

Keep in mind, you always carry anything God encounters you with. So the prophetic just stays with you; it's what we operate in. But for quite a while now we've been operating more and more in the apostolic. We've been building and planting and usurping and taking ground, and it's a lot of what we do even now with discipling, training, and crusades. But that encounter was instilled back in 2011, and it takes time to play out at times.

When seeking out understanding on these California/Virginia experiences, I prayed, "God, why did I have to wait until Virginia to manifest this light that I now have forever as an experience?" He showed me that what had happened was that I triggered that region because Virginia is the gateway to our nation, really. We know that the Native Americans were here first, but with what we now walk in in the birthing of a nation and the colonies that made things official in the US, it all was birthed in Virginia. It's the gateway to our nation, the region it was birthed. That's what happened to show me even the call to a people here in the US. Once I got into that area, it triggered the manifestation of this same commissioning.

We see a lot of wonders and encounters in many places around the world, don't get me wrong, but for a while it was as if the more "out there" wonders were only happening in the United States. Don't get me wrong, heaven is heaven, and when you're called to a place, God's authority is with you. But we just had a greater landing of it in the US. When you are called to a certain place, you think, *no wonder when I go into this nation, there's such ease and authority and doors open and platforms are available to me.* In fact, in some cases you may have to dial it back some. I have to do that very often, to be honest with you. I'm in South America a lot on crusades, and who we really fully are, I often have to dial back, and that's okay. I'll be all things to all people, but we have to just redirect all of these facets you may see us in for the sake of where we are ministering.

My journey was just the prophetic for a long time, and you never lose it, but then it overlapped more into the apostolic, planting, and building. Paul was very similar. He was really an apostolic prophet. He could flow in all five, but the two main offshoots of who he was, was an apostle with a strong prophetic/revelatory anointing. The Lord has brought me into specific commissioning, empowering, and revelatory encounters to direct these steps along the way. I didn't go after the calling specifically; I went after Him. I went after the encounter. It's Him who gets to decide what the encounter will birth and what destiny I'll be launched into.

WHIRLWINDS

I honestly can't recall what year this next encounter happened, but chronologically it was after the falcon encounter I mentioned earlier. The reason I know this is because I was having visions and dreams regularly at this point. I was waiting on the Lord and I got taken into a vision where I saw these huge tornados, both equal in stature, spinning and coming at me. They were massive; I could see these power lines and trees that looked like little Monopoly pieces. That's how huge these tornadoes were. And this vision, thank goodness, had the interpretation already in it. That doesn't always happen.

Most often we're like Peter in Acts 10, who saw a sheet coming down three times, mysteries, symbols, and if you read closely, it says Peter then pondered upon what the vision might have meant. He didn't know what it meant, and then the Holy Spirit spoke to him. Like we've already established, as you ponder it and lean in, then *revelation* comes. You know the interpretation to some dreams and visions as they play out, but very rarely does it happen this way. Thank God this was one of those.

In the vision of these two tornadoes, I knew the one on the left was revelation, and the one on the right was power. It was almost like they were wearing name tags. I just knew these tornadoes were whirlwinds. As they came toward me and got closer, they merged into each other and formed one huge tornado and got even bigger, and then hit me. Then I got taken out of my body, and I could see myself like a rag doll get thrown around in this tornado and get sucked around. Then all of the sudden, this huge whirlwind spit me out, and shot me straight up to Pennsylvania, of all places. As soon as I hit Pennsylvania, it was like I was a pinball, bouncing around from state to state all over this nation, and then the nations of the world. Then I came out of the vision.

It was so profound, I never forgot it. I always knew from this vision that something with my commission in revelation and power would have to go through Pennsylvania. There's a real commissioning element there; Global Awakening and other ministries; and there's a real pioneering element there as well. From the vision I knew there was something really important with Pennsylvania. Years passed as I ministered and went to different places, flowing in the prophetic ministry and all. Yet I knew something big was supposed to happen and go through Pennsylvania.

About seven years passed after this particular vision. Sometimes we can look at these things and think, *why doesn't God just tell us something straight up instead of getting our hopes up for so long?* But He knows precisely when, where, and how to tell us something. It's all in His perfect timing, and He knows what to give you to get you to hang on through different seasons.

I received an invitation to go speak in Pennsylvania, at Randy Clark's School of the Supernatural at Global Awakening. When I got the invite, I knew that *this was it*. I didn't tell anybody, but I was excited. The day came where I was to fly out, and I received a call from somebody while I was on the treadmill at the gym that knew I was flying out that day. This person asked me, "Hey Brian, did you see what's going on with all the whirlwinds and tornadoes?" I had not, and told this person I didn't even watch the weather. He told me there'd been a huge weather band of tornadoes starting down right here in Louisiana and was concerned about whether I'd be able to fly out that day.

I went and checked the weather after this call, and there wasn't even a blip of anything all over the rest of the United States. The whole country was crystal clear on this particular day. No tornado anywhere. Except this day, there was this crazy band of tornadoes and whirlwinds that went from Louisiana all the way up to Pennsylvania. The exact track I saw in the vision seven years earlier of this whirlwind shooting me out and spitting me out in Pennsylvania. I took a screenshot of this to keep in my journal as a remembrance of this.

So I connected through Atlanta on my way up, watching the weather closely, and that band just continued going up all the way to Pennsylvania. Thank goodness they didn't cancel our flights, but it was a sign and wonder, and the meetings up at Global Awakening were really powerful. They are a commissioning-apostolic type of hub, in a sense, and now since that time I'm up there with a group almost once a year.

I love that region, but you have to watch heaven on these things. And since then too, the catapulting of course in increasing and going to the nations has really taken off in our ministry. God will mark the atmosphere with signs, but you also want to watch these things in a real profound way.

You'll see a lot of what your call is in these encounters, as we've said.

So the falcon was more prophetic, and the blinding light is obviously more of an apostolic, and the Lord even showed me a people group by the time it triggered by photo. It's just really key and there's a lot of weight on the installment of how God has a run-in with you.

I just want to encourage you to press in for it, but also dissect the past ones you've had to the fullest if you haven't already. A lot will unfold for you as you do because it's who God is.

You even see whirlwinds would always follow William Branham from a young age when God would speak out of whirlwinds. He had the spirit of Elijah on him, and although it's not documented that he ever said he was Elijah, all of that got twisted and used against him. But he came in the spirit of Elijah, which was whirlwinds. So you have to watch the way in which God encounters you. Whirlwinds in all of Scripture tie back to Elijah, and it's the very spirit Branham flowed in.

Solomon had a dream and God came to him. There was no mysterious fire or angel with a sword or a blinding light mystery. God asked him what he wanted. This is the first major encounter He had with him, and Solomon said he wanted wisdom that he may govern God's Kingdom. It got granted to him. Of course, what was Solomon known for in all of history? Wisdom. He wrote the Proverbs, Ecclesiastes, and was the wisest man put on the earth. The first encounter he had with the Lord branded him for who he was.

WHETHER IT'S AN ENCOUNTER FROM THE SCRIPTURES OR AN encounter from my own life, may you be inspired to chase this experiential God in a new way. May faith from the biblical foundation and hunger for the powerful results be birthed in your heart. Whether it's a commissioning encounter, an empowering encounter, a revelatory encounter, or a repositioning encounter, may you be impacted by it in an irreversible way. May you dissect encounters of old and take hold of new ones and be forever changed as a result. Divine encounters are not a mere added benefit of our walk with Jesus, but the bedrock of our walk with Jesus. May we chase them accordingly.

PRAYER FOR ENCOUNTERS

∽

"Lord, I thank You for encounters. Whether it's a commissioning encounter, an empowering encounter, a revelatory encounter, or a repositioning encounter, thank You for manifesting them to Your people. I pray for fresh illumination on Your people. I ask for fresh revelation to enlighten those experiences that they would even come back into fresh recollection of those experiences they've had with You and recognize the call and realize their destiny.

I pray even now for fresh commissioning encounters upon the readers all across the world, in every nation, state, and every home. I pray for a fresh wind to blow, a fresh wind of encounters. Teach us, Lord, to dissect and reap the full benefit of past encounters while opening ourselves to new ones from You, in Jesus' name. Amen."

ABOUT THE AUTHOR

Brian Guerin is the founding president of Bridal Glory International. He graduated from the Brownsville School of Ministry/F.I.R.E. in 2001, and now travels throughout the U.S. and the world teaching and preaching the gospel of the Lord Jesus Christ. Brian has appeared on T.B.N. and GOD-TV and currently hosts his own broadcasting channel on YouTube. He also authored two previously released books, *Modern Day Mysticism* and *God of Wonders*. His main passion and emphasis in life is to draw the Bride of Christ into greater intimacy with the Bridegroom Himself-Jesus Christ, leading to the maturity of the Bride and the culmination of His glorious return. Brian also enjoys bringing great emphasis and depth to the art of hearing the voice of God through dreams, visions, signs, and wonders.

VISIT BRIDAL GLORY ON THE WEB & SOCIAL:
WWW.BRIDALGLORY.COM

SOCIAL: @BRIDALGLORY

Made in the USA
Middletown, DE
14 April 2019